A Discourse Perspective on *Bunreacht na hÉireann*

A Discourse Perspective on *Bunreacht na Éireann*:

A Sound Constitution?

By

Davide Mazzi

Cambridge Scholars Publishing

A Discourse Perspective on *Bunreacht na hÉireann*: A Sound Constitution?

By Davide Mazzi

This book first published 2020

Cambridge Scholars Publishing

Lady Stephenson Library, Newcastle upon Tyne, NE6 2PA, UK

British Library Cataloguing in Publication Data
A catalogue record for this book is available from the British Library

ISBN (10): 1-5275-5589-5
ISBN (13): 978-1-5275-5589-1

"It is true that the Constitution is a legal document, but it is a fundamental one which establishes the State and it expresses not only legal norms but basic doctrines of political and social theory".

O'Higgins, C.J., 1976

TABLE OF CONTENTS

List of Figures and Tables

ACKNOWLEDGMENTS

The idea of writing a book about the Irish Constitution dates back a few years, during a period of research leave at the National Library of Ireland, as ever a source of inspiration. We all agree that constitutions play a fundamental role in the legal order of the countries where a founding charter was drafted and adopted. Likewise, it is well known that constitutional texts have already been investigated by a wide range of scholars including political scientists and legal theorists. However, I was eager to know more about the language of Ireland's *Bunreacht* as well as its presence in Irish public discourse over the 80 years of its existence. In an attempt to design and complete a research project aimed at combining a variety of approaches within an original work, this volume took shape after crucial research periods at the National Library of Ireland (January 2018, 2019 and 2020) and the Boole Library at University College Cork (October 2018 and September 2019). I would like to express heartfelt gratitude to the staff of both libraries and to that of my own university library (*Biblioteca Umanistica*, University of Modena and Reggio Emilia), which also provided materials highly relevant to this project.

Chapter One

The Constitution of Ireland (*Bunreacht na hÉireann*): A Preliminary Overview

1.1 What this book is

There is undoubtedly something fascinating about constitutions. As a set of fundamental principles that form the basis of a polity, they are commonly designed to determine how that polity is to be governed. For this reason, constitutions tell us something about the shared values cherished by nations who adopt them. With the exception of authoritarian regimes, where constitutions exist yet only nominally, the founding charters drafted in liberal-democratic communities have a normative character. They are intended to govern the political process, while at the same time reflecting the traditions, culture and standards of a country. As such, a constitution tends precisely to be judged "by the extent to which it gives a comparatively clear account of the governmental system as it actually operates, together with a fair idea of the aims which governments do in fact pursue and of the limits" within which governments elect to confine themselves (Chubb 1991, 6).

As we know them, constitutions are a product of the modern world. As Chubb (1991) points out, the seventeenth century was the period in which the idea of a document building a framework of government began to be entertained. As a by-product of liberalism and its disdain for the concentration of absolute power and its arbitrary nature, constitutions were then to develop in Western Europe and North America in the attempt to define and delimit government. The term "constitutionalism" itself ought to be set against the background of the deep-seated belief that the rule of law should be implemented on the basis of principles enshrined in a fundamental law along the following lines: first of all, the separation of powers; secondly, the notion that governments should not simply enforce the law, but also abide by it themselves.

In Federalist Paper No. 50, James Madison (1787, 285) argued that "in framing a government", the "great difficulty lies in this: you must first enable the government to control the governed; and in the next place oblige it to control itself. A dependence on the people is, no doubt, the primary control on the government". This reference to "the people" adds a further feature to modern constitutionalist views, namely the requirement that sovereignty lie in the hands of citizens. Taken together, popular sovereignty and liberal doctrines have formed the core of constitutionalism since the eighteenth century. They therefore served as a basis for the normative constitutions enacted by European countries, to which the Republic of Ireland has been no exception.

By reason of their significance for the countries where they are in force, constitutions may be approached from various perspectives: one is political theory, as in the last few paragraphs, while another is legal theory, in order to account for the system of checks and balances introduced by a charter. In this book, a different angle is taken on the matter. As its object of study, the Constitution of Ireland will be investigated from a discourse perspective. This means that, to begin with, its language is analysed. Secondly, its impact on the Irish public sphere is assessed at different levels. In particular, the volume fields the following research questions: (1) Why has the Constitution (in Irish, the first official language of the State, *Bunreacht na hÉireann*) been such a key document for the Republic?; (2) What was (/is) the impact of the Constitution on Irish public discourse at both a popular and a specialised level?; and, more specifically, (3) How was the Constitution represented and "argued" by the Irish press upon its enactment?; (4) How has it entered the argumentation of Irish judges across the decades, as they have been required to pronounce on the compatibility of proposed legislation with its norms?

The first of these questions is addressed in this chapter, which aims at providing a brief account of the specificity of *Bunreacht na hÉireann*, its constitutive elements and even its controversial aspects. The rest of the book discusses the remaining three questions by combining analytical insights of different kinds, and from both a quantitative and a qualitative point of view. The integrated approach adopted here is therefore intended to explore the relationship between the text of the *Bunreacht* and the polity it has been designed to serve, by using tools other than those customarily developed for the study of fundamental laws so far.

1.2 *Bunreacht na hÉireann*: A short history

From a historical point of view, it would be quite incorrect to say that *Bunreacht na hÉireann* was Independent Ireland's first constitution. After 26 of Ireland's 32 counties won Independence in 1922, the newly-formed Irish Free State adopted a Constitution, i.e. *Bunreacht Shaorstáit Éireann* [Constitution of the Irish Free State] (Cahillane 2011). Its origins lay in the Anglo-Irish Treaty of December 1921 and the imminent British threats of war immediate and terrible (Kee 2000 [1972]), should the Irish people decline to accept the terms of agreement and the Constitution itself as urged by the then Secretary of State for the Dominions, Winston Churchill.

The British pressure was apparent from those articles that secured the appointment of a Governor-General as the representative of the Crown, and included the introduction of an Oath of Allegiance to HM King George V, his heirs and successors. In addition, *Bunreacht Shaorstáit Éireann* declared the Free State to be part of the British Commonwealth of Nations, while it instituted the *Seanad* as an upper house designed to guarantee effective representation to the Protestant minority. Finally, the opening section of the Act establishing the Constitution clearly stated that, if any of its provision were, "even after the British government's officers had scrutinised the document with a fine-tooth comb, in conflict with the Anglo-Irish Treaty", that provision would be deemed void and inoperative (Gallagher 2005, 73).

Soon after Independence (1923), the Free State joined the League of Nations. Between 1926 and 1929, moreover, it championed the cause of independence at imperial conferences, thereby making a meaningful contribution to shaping policy that was to result in the Statute of Westminster in 1931. A far-reaching effect of the Statute was to remove nearly all of the British Parliament's authority to legislate for the Dominions and, consequently, turn these into largely sovereign nations. It was a crucial step in the development of the Dominions as separate States in their own right.

The year 1932 would then turn out to be a political turning point for the emerging State, when Eamon de Valera's *Fianna Fáil* party first came to power. De Valera was to become a prominent figure in twentieth-century Irish politics, serving for many years as *Taoiseach* [Prime Minister] and twice as the Irish President. A former doctrinaire republican and anti-Treaty militant, he was resolutely opposed to the Constitution, which he saw as an imposition rather than a document in line with the aspirations of a free and proud people. When his party was returned with the majority it needed to form a new government supported by the Labour Party, it began by furthering a protectionist agenda, whereby "self-sufficiency became the ultimate objective of Irish economic policy" (Press 1986, 74). A year later, after the *Seanad* delayed provisions to abolish the Oath, de Valera dissolved the *Dáil* (the State's lower House) to seek a strong popular mandate to use democratic means to dismantle the Free State's Dominion status.

In the 1933 general election, *Fianna Fáil* won enough seats to form a government without Labour support, so that de Valera was in a position to pursue his radical agenda more comfortably. Even after he ensured the abolition of the Oath of Allegiance along with the office of Governor General and the *Seanad* itself, he "remained adamant that if the Irish people wanted a truly legitimate basic law then it would have to come ultimately from themselves" (Keogh and McCarthy 2007, 62). His concerns were as much with the current Constitution's main contents as with the circumstances in which the document had been drafted. Content-wise, de Valera saw it as a flimsy paper barrier that could hardly prevent the government of the day from eroding civil liberties as it pleased. With regard to its genesis, he genuinely believed that Ireland's national sentiments jarred with a Constitution that ultimately went back to a Treaty he had never recognised as legitimate.

In 1934, therefore, he set up a constitutional committee, and during the *Dáil* debate on the abolition of the *Seanad* of 1936, he said his hope was to have a draft document ready by the following autumn. The impulse to abolish the *Seanad* seems to have been the catalyst to initiate the process as the committee duly published a report. This was followed by the draft heads, before the project was fully implemented and completed with the circulation of a draft to the cabinet and government departments. This was then debated in the *Dáil* and submitted to the people for approval. The plebiscite was held on the same day as a general election, and the new Constitution was approved by 57% of the electorate, a somewhat narrow margin due to a vote largely splitting along political lines (Daly 2020). *Bunreacht na hÉireann* came into force on 29 December 1937.

1.3 *Bunreacht na hÉireann*: Distinctive aspects

In the Republic of Ireland as well as in many other countries, respect for the law and its binding force are crucial to the effective and equitable operation of democratic government. In the Irish jurisdiction, the law judges are called upon to interpret and apply is essentially threefold. First of all, the common law and equity, which can be broadly defined as law resulting from judicial decisions accumulating over the years; secondly, statute law, which refers to legislation enacted by the *Oireachtas* [Parliament]; finally, and perhaps most importantly, the Constitution, which has a higher legal status than other legal sources, with one notable exception: as in other European Union Member States, EU law takes precedence over national law.

Despite the primacy of EU law, the Constitution of Ireland has constantly been regarded as both the fundamental law of the land and a kind of higher law for several reasons. One is that the *Bunreacht* is superior to all other types of national law, whether public or private: accordingly, it "controls the statute law and the common law, to the extent that where either of these conflict with the Constitution they are unenforceable and void. In the case of any such conflict arising, the courts must apply the superior" law, i.e. the Constitution itself (Walsh 1988, 191). One more reason is that the Constitution may not be altered or repealed "in the manner of ordinary legislation, for besides the approval of both Houses of the *Oireachtas*, such changes require the consent of the majority of the electors at a referendum" (Chubb 1991, 1).

Bunreacht na hÉireann opens with a clear and solemn declaration of independence and right to self-determination, as is the case with many other constitutional texts: "The Irish nation," so Article 1 goes, "hereby affirms its inalienable, indefeasible, and sovereign right to choose its own form of Government, to determine its relations with other nations, and to develop its life, political, economic and cultural, in accordance with its own genius and traditions" (2018 [1937], 4).[1] Such an assertion was largely predictable from a text designed to mark out a basic law that was a sharp departure from its antecedent.

More contentious, nonetheless, was the early version of Articles 2 and 3. The original wording of Article 2 was that the national territory of Ireland consisted "of the whole island of Ireland, its islands and the territorial seas" (1937, 4). The effect of this bold assertion might appear to

---

[1] It is important to note that in this chapter, more than one version of the Constitution is referred to. On the one hand, the passages taken from the *Bunreacht* in its current form are dated as *(2018 [1937])*, in order to highlight that the most recent edition of the Constitution was used, while at the same time acknowledging the year of its enactment. On the other hand, the extracts from the earliest version are simply dated as *(1937)*. Finally, on the only occasion the Constitution of the Irish Free State Act is quoted from, the relevant passage is dated as *(1936 [1922])*, because a 1936 edition of the 1922 document was used. In the rest of the volume, only the *Bunreacht* in its current form is cited. As a result, no information is reported other than the specific articles from which examples are taken.

have been mitigated by the text of Article 3, which stated that the laws enacted by the *Oireachtas* would only apply to the area to be identified with the Irish Free State and have the same extra-territorial effect. However, the purpose of this proviso was itself defeated by the premise that this would be the case "[p]ending the re-integration of the national territory, and without prejudice to the right of the Parliament and Government established by this Constitution to exercise jurisdiction over the whole of that territory" (1937, 4).

As was to be expected, the two articles caused considerable irritation in those in Northern Ireland holding a Unionist viewpoint opposed to a nationalist view of the Irish nation. Upon the signing of the Good Friday Agreement of April 1998, the claim that the national territory of the Republic of Ireland was inclusive of Northern Ireland was dropped and replaced by the acknowledgment that the six counties of the North form part of the United Kingdom of Great Britain and Northern Ireland and are subject to a separate jurisdiction. As we will see in Chapter 4, when Article 2 is taken as an example during our analysis of the language of the *Bunreacht*, the focus of the new provisions is less on a definition of the national territory than on the people of Ireland, their close ties to the land and the recognition of the "diversity of their identities and traditions" (2018 [1937], 4).

While the first part of the Constitution is mainly concerned with the sovereignty of the people as the source of all legal authority and describes the institutions of the State (Byrne et al. 2014), the second part of it mainly deals with the fundamental rights of persons. In this important respect, the Irish Constitution differs from the British model: "that is the fact that it incorporates what is sometimes called a 'bill of rights', in other words a set of statements about citizens' fundamental rights and liberties, which the parliament is not entitled to cut down" through ordinary legislation (Kelly 1988, 163). Many of the fundamental rights are contained in Articles 40-44, even though other articles confer equally important rights.

On the one hand, some rights are explicitly recognised and asserted: among these, to mention but a few, the right to an inviolable dwelling not to be entered forcibly, save in accordance with law (Art. 40.5); the right to educate children, subject to limited rights of the State (Art. 42); the right to own private property (Art. 43) and, most notably, that not to be deprived of one's liberty save in accordance with law (Art. 40.4). This last provision is a cornerstone of the rule of law in free and democratic countries, and jurists refer to the cardinal principle it embraces as *habeas corpus*. Although the term is not mentioned in the Constitution, the wording of Article 40.4 lends substance to it. It is the mechanism triggered to both challenge the legality of a detention and discover any flaw or irregularity in it. As Professor Kelly (1994 [1961], 897), a most respected authority on the *Bunreacht*, pointed out,

> [t]he form taken by the procedure is, briefly, that the party complaining of unlawful detention applies ex parte for, and as a rule automatically gets, a[n] initial order directed to the person alleged to be detaining him–typically, the governor of a prison–and calling on that person to appear and justify the detention. If, on that appearance, that person fails to justify the detention, the initial order is made absolute and the person the subject of the application is ordered to be released. If on the other hand the lawfulness of the detention is established to the Court's satisfaction, the initial order is 'discharged'.

As Byrne et al. (2014, 726) observe, few of these rights "are absolute in nature" and to a certain extent, it is incumbent on courts in constitutional judicial review "to determine the precise meaning of the general limits placed on such rights".

On the other hand, Article 40.3, which will be highly relevant to our study of judicial argumentation in Chapter 6, has constituted an additional source of rights over the past few decades. In the 1950s, barely twenty years since the Constitution was enacted, fundamental rights had been asserted by Irish courts only in a minority of cases. A turning point in the country's judicial history was Cearbhall Ó Dálaigh's appointment to Chief Justice of the Supreme Court in 1961, along with Justices Brian Walsh and John Kenny to the Supreme Court and High Court, respectively. These judges epitomised a judicial generation that was to bring about nothing short of a revolution in Irish constitutional jurisprudence. In Kelly's own words (1988, 167-168),

> [t]he most spectacular conquest of that revolution was the recognition–which an earlier generation of judges would have though fantastic–that the Constitution implicitly protected an indefinite range of citizens' rights over and above those specifically enumerated in one or other article, and that the courts were entitled to identify such latent rights, whenever the occasion arose, by reference to their understanding of a standard such as 'the Christian and democratic nature of the State'.

The "latent rights" Kelly wrote about were to go down in history as "unenumerated rights", since there is no comprehensive list of the rights generated under the general terms of Article 40.3. The way such striking development unfolded was through cases such as *Ryan v. Attorney General* [1965] IR 294 and *McGee v. Attorney General* [1974] IR 284.

The proceedings in the former were instigated by Mrs Gladys Ryan, who challenged the constitutionality of the Health (Fluoridation of Water Supplies) Act, 1960. Mrs Ryan was a member of a group opposing the new practice of adding sodium fluoride to the public water supply. Briefly, a Consultative Council appointed by the Government had presented a report in which the addition of limited amounts of the substance to water supplies was said to contribute substantially to reduce tooth decay. As a result, the Act was introduced to enable local authorities to add specified quantities of sodium fluoride to public water supplies throughout the State. Although the report was based on the most recently available scientific evidence on the matter, Mrs Ryan brought an action against the State. In particular, she alleged that this treatment of the water supply constituted a serious infringement of her (and her children's) right to "bodily integrity", on the grounds that she and her family would henceforward be obliged to consume water containing a substance that may have posed public health risks.

Interestingly, the Constitution says nothing about "bodily integrity", which her counsel associated with a right to be free from any action imposed by the State resulting in harm to anyone's life or health. By contrast, the *Bunreacht* defends and guarantees "the personal rights of the citizen" (Art. 40.3.1). Within such a framework, Mrs Ryan's counsel pointed out that a thorough understanding of the phrase "personal rights" implied going far beyond traditional civil liberties such as freedom from arbitrary arrest, freedom of speech and of the press and others. Personal rights, they insisted in spite of the difficulty in pleading their client's case, should also include the right not to have potentially poisonous water forced upon you by the State.

In what would be seen as a landmark judgment, Justice Kenny acknowledged that the water fluoridation introduced by the Act was by all means harmless. Yet he agreed with Mrs Ryan's counsel that citizens' personal rights are not limited to the letter of the constitutional text. Remarkably, he added that it would be a matter for the High Court to bring to light and enforce such unspecified rights, no matter if that involved occasionally militating against Acts of the *Oireachtas*. Chief Justice Ó Dálaigh's Supreme Court also concluded that water fluoridation might even be beneficial, but it reiterated Justice Kenny's point of principle, "thus making Mrs Ryan's case into a sort of floodgate for assertions of personal rights claimed to be latent in the Constitution" (Kelly 1988, 168).

The distinct echo of the assertion of unenumerated rights also reverberated in a sequence of cases concerning various aspects of sexuality and the right of privacy, as could be appreciated from *McGee v. Attorney*

General. The plaintiff, Mrs McGee, was a married woman who had been advised by her doctor that any further pregnancy would pose extreme danger to her life. For this reason, she and her husband decided to use a method of contraception. Based on her doctor's advice, she opted for spermicidal jelly, which should have been imported into the State. However, this was impounded by the Revenue Commissioners in accordance with the Criminal Law Amendment Act, 1935, which laid down that importation of contraceptives was a criminal offence. In its judgment, the Supreme Court upheld the plaintiff's right to import contraceptives for her own private use. The law that forbade this, the Court held, was in flagrant violation of her right to "marital privacy".

Ever since the verdict in the Ryan case, therefore, a whole string of unspecified personal rights have been upheld by the Irish courts. These include, but are not limited to, the right not to be tortured or ill-treated, the right to travel outside the State, the right of access to the courts, to legal representation in criminal cases, to fair procedures and to know the identity of one's natural mother (Byrne et al. 2014, 728). This clarifies that the range of matters covered by the protection enshrined in Article 40.3 is indeed very wide. Nevertheless, it is important to note that, like those expressly stated in the Constitution, these rights are not absolute. Conversely, they are to some extent qualified by the requirement that the State must defend them "as far as practicable" (2018 [1937], 154). As early as in *Ryan v. Attorney General*, accordingly, both the High Court and the Supreme Court were satisfied that the right to bodily integrity was protected by Article 40.3. At the same time, they ruled that the State could not be established to have failed to affirm it in the Health (Fluoridation of Water Supplies) Act, 1960, so that Mrs Ryan's challenge to its constitutionality was eventually unsuccessful.

The doctrine of unenumerated rights has met strenuous objections over the years. The list of such rights has been revealed by jurisprudence to be open. It would therefore seem that any citizen feeling that a personal right unmentioned in the black-and-white text of the Constitution has been denied may still succeed in having it enforced by the courts, as long as these are persuaded that that right is in some way necessarily implied by the "Christian and democratic nature of the State". In principle, one might contend that rights such as marital privacy appear nowhere in the *Bunreacht* precisely because it was not the intention of the people in 1937 to safeguard them. On the other hand, it has been retorted that "no interpretation of the Constitution is intended to be final for all time. It is given in the light of prevailing ideas and concepts" (Walsh J. in Byrne et al. 2014, 756). It goes without saying that all sorts of difficulties may arise in determining the nature of "prevailing ideas and concepts". This raises the fundamental issue of how to interpret the Constitution, which is discussed in the following section.

1.4 The challenges of constitutional interpretation

In *McGee v. Attorney General*, Justice O'Keeffe argued that "fundamental constitutional values could be conditioned by passage of time", and added that "no interpretation of the Constitution is intended to be final for all time" (in Hogan 1987, 175). In this matter, Walsh and O'Keeffe JJ. march in unison, as it were. Indeed, the fact that they use the exact same words–*no interpretation [...] is intended to be final for all time*–reinforces the idea that constitutional interpretation may pose formidable challenges to every generation's judiciary.

In the main, written constitutions contain detailed provisions applying to elections and appointments of various kinds, which may be understood literally and unambiguously. In their capacity as fundamental laws, however, they invariably frame abstract, normative concepts to articulate principles intended to protect fundamental rights. Examples include *common good* (Art. 6.1), *public morality* (Artt. 40.6.1 and 44.2.1), *family* (Art. 41.1.1) and *natural rights* (Art. 43.1.1). By virtue of their open-ended meaning and theory-laden nature, these are the terms Clarke (2008) discusses as "essentially contested" concepts. In Clarke's view (2008, 113), their presence in constitutional text is postulated to require that

> in addition to the text as their first source of authority–Irish courts of appeal interpret the Constitution in the light of fundamental principles of justice that have been developed over centuries; that such principles are "transcendent" in the relevant sense; that the occurrence of essentially contested concepts in the Constitution is symptomatic of its normative character; and that such concepts need to be interpreted anew, in each generation, with due fidelity to the principles that they were meant to articulate.

So what are the canons to interpret such concepts, and the constitutional text more generally? First of all, a "literal or grammatical approach" has been applied by the courts and was prevalent in the 1960s and 1970s. As we will appreciate from Chapter 2 (Subsection 2.5.3), this approach is comparable to that adopted in the interpretation of legislation. Whether in a statutory or in a constitutional context, this approach can be justified on the grounds that courts stay faithful to the text of the materials under scrutiny. As a result, they do not draw criticism for substituting personal or subjective judgment for more objective determinations.

Secondly, those judges who are sceptical about judicial activism and liberalism have echoed a sentiment expressed at times by the United States Supreme Court as well. By this approach, judges should strive to find an original understanding, as it were, of constitutional text, in keeping with the views of those who drafted it. In the Republic of Ireland, this has implied referring to well-established principles of law or the state of the law in 1937, when *Bunreacht na hÉireann* was introduced. Looking at the original framers' intentions underlies what is known as a "historical approach".

In third place, emphasis has been laid on the need to make sure that each provision is interpreted not in isolation, but in a way that contextualises it in the general constitutional order. This is known as a "harmonious approach" (Doyle 2008), which requires courts to read provisions as is consistent with the overall scheme of the constitution. It is a purposive approach geared to avoid internal inconsistency between one norm and the next. A persuasive definition of the underlying interpretive technique is provided by Costello J., who asserted that, "whilst not ignoring the express text of the Constitution," such a broad approach "would look at the whole text of the Constitution and identify its purpose and objectives", as is desirable "in protecting fundamental rights" (in Hogan 1987, 185). The harmonious approach has been observed to be identical with that pursued by the Court of Justice of the European Union as it interprets the treaties underpinning European Union law and its principles. This is suggested by Byrne et al. (2014, 759) to bear witness to the substantial influence of EU law on Irish interpretative techniques.

Fourthly, the Constitution has been approached from the angle of natural law. In Article 41.1, family is recognised by the State "as a moral institution possessing inalienable and imprescriptible rights, antecedent and superior to all positive law" (2018 [1937], 162). Behind norms such as this is the notion that citizens enjoy a number of rights by reason of their human personality. This is commonly referred to as "natural law", as opposed and superior to "positive law", namely the law of human institutions such as parliaments. The view of natural law advocates is that such rights are inalienable in that individuals may not give them away; they are imprescriptible, so that they may not be taken away by the State; and they are antecedent to positive law because they pre-date it in some pre-existing form. Examples include equality before the law, protected by Article 40.1.

The difficulties in approaching the Constitution by underlining the superiority of natural law are essentially twofold. To begin with, the full scope of natural rights may be hard to determine. In addition, current thinking about them is likely to change over time. As Byrne et al. (2014, 762) highlight, "some philosophers have criticized the natural law tradition for its lack of specificity", while the obvious connection of natural law with Christian philosophy and the Roman Catholic Church more specifically "has resulted in a negative response from philosophers who espouse a secular approach to the content of law".

In light of the diversity and complexity of the four main approaches summarised here, there might be a temptation to ask whether any particular theory or method of constitutional interpretation has been applied by Irish courts on a steadier basis. Scholars such as Hogan (1987) and Morgan (2001) appear to suggest that none in particular has. This seeming lack of consistency has been deemed "so prevalent that individual judges have from time to time adopted different approaches to this question, utilising whatever method might seem to be most convenient or to offer adventitious support for conclusions" they have already drawn (Hogan 1987, 187).

This sounds like a fairly harsh judgment, but the fact remains that the question of the approach(es) to be adopted for the interpretation of the Constitution is set to remain difficult and controversial. In order to uncover the reasons behind this, it should be borne in mind that the *Bunreacht* was in no way drafted in the same way, or with the same aim, as ordinary legislation. This is so, Morgan (1998, 114-115) explains, because the Constitution "covers an unimaginably broader span than any statute: it deals with nothing less than the organs of government and, secondly, the fundamental rights, in other words the relationship between the individual and ordered society".

At the outset, constitutional interpretation may be assumed to be the most controversial aspect worth examining in relation to the Irish Constitution. While this has been brought to the fore by scholarly research, it is arguably not the only one. Others include the conceptualisation of women, the influence of religion and the Catholic Church, and language issues, which are respectively discussed in Sections 1.5, 1.6 and 1.7 below.

1.5 *Bunreacht na hÉireann* and women

In Article 3 of the Free State Constitution, a declaration of sexual equality before the law had been made. By contrast, no corresponding article was included in the 1937 draft of *Bunreacht na hÉireann*. Such glaring omission, it was objected, could result in a loss of the right to vote or even citizenship. This seemed to be the case especially when the conspicuous absence of the phrase "without distinction of sex" (1936 [1922], 34) was read in conjunction with Article 40.1. This holds that, whereas all citizens are "equal before the law", due regard is had "to differences of capacity, physical and moral, and of social function" (2018 [1937], 152). Could this not be used by any unscrupulous government, some asked, to trample on women's rights? That a close examination of the new Constitution begged the question is confirmed by the formulation of Article 41.2.1-2 (2018 [1937], 164), which reads as follows:

> 1° In particular, the state recognises that by her life **within the home**, woman gives to the state a support without which the common good cannot be achieved.
> 2° The state shall, therefore, endeavour to ensure that **mothers** shall not be obliged by economic necessity to engage in labour to the neglect of **their duties in the home**. [My emphasis]

The somewhat narrow conception of women as *mothers*, rather than *citizens* in their own right, along with the emphasis laid on *the home* as their natural environment, would draw intense criticism from women themselves. In a letter to de Valera published by the *Irish Press*, Louie Bennett, Secretary of the Irish Women's Workers Union, contended that the draft constitution contained points of "serious danger" for the "implications that may be given to them" no less than "for what they actually state" (in Keogh and McCarthy 2007, 186). Furthermore, she recommended that the wording of Article 41.2.1 should be changed from *her life within the home* into *her work for the home*, in open acknowledgement of the value of women's work in a broad field and for the common good.

Ms Bennett's recommendations were duly ignored, while the controversial academic Alfred O'Rahilly referred to her as "Lady Bountiful" and dismissed her claims as "hypercritical if not slightly hysterical" (in Keogh and McCarthy 2007, 186). De Valera later accepted to meet with representatives from women's organisations, the joint committee of women's societies and social workers and the National University Women Graduates' Association, among others. Even though he was pleased to let them articulate their concerns over legislation resulting from the Constitution that would discriminate against women in relation to citizenship and the franchise, the meetings remained essentially non-committal.

In their in-depth analysis of contemporary documents, Keogh and McCarthy (2007, 187) draw the attention to three papal encyclicals as the source of the principles that were eventually embraced by the *Bunreacht*. In Leo XIII's *Rerum Novarum*, first of all, the view is aired that women were unsuited for certain occupations. In Pius XI's *Quadragesimo Anno*, secondly, the Pontiff urged society to discourage women's engagement in gainful occupations beyond the domestic walls as a form of "abuse" resulting in the "neglect of their own proper cares and duties". In third place, Pius XI's *Casti Connubii* insisted that woman should be the "mistress of the home", whereas men ought to devote themselves to work. As a devout Catholic, it hardly comes as a surprise that de Valera's own words would echo the same views. In particular, while addressing the *Dáil* on 11 May 1937, these are the words he used in the matter of women in the Constitution (in Moynihan 1980, 324):

> With regard to women, they are mentioned in two articles. But why are they mentioned? They are mentioned to give the protection which, I think, is necessary as part of our social programme, and I am prepared to go with that programme before the country. I do not care what criticism comes from anybody on the basis of it. We state here [Article 41.2] that mothers in their homes give to the State a support which is essential. Is there anybody who denies it? Is it not a tribute to the work that is done by women in the homes as mothers? […] In regard to labour and in regard to work, our aim ought to be–we may be too slow in arriving at it, but no country has apparently done it yet–that **the breadwinner**, **who is normally and naturally** in these cases, when he is alive, **the father of the family**, should be able by his work to bring in enough to maintain the whole household and that women ought not to be forced by economic necessity to go out and either supplement his wages or become the breadwinners themselves. [My emphasis]

It is a fact that women played no part in framing the Constitution. Of the 152 TDs (Irish MPs) who might have had a chance to comment on the draft, only three were women. However, none of them contributed in any meaningful way to the debate on the draft. By reading through the extensive quote from de Valera's speech earlier on, one may agree with Scannell (1988, 123) that he was neither a feminist nor by any extent consciously anti-women: rather, "his views reflected those of most people in Irish society at the time", while they "certainly accorded with those of nearly all of the deputies who spoke in the Dáil".

Indeed, by looking at the wording of Article 41.2.1-2 and at the same time taking de Valera at his word, the text of the *Bunreacht* is open to two interpretations. The first is to consider the opening paragraph of the Article as a tribute to the work undertaken by women in the home in their capacity as mothers. Consistent with this, the second paragraph would then read as offering women constitutional protection from the *economic necessity* of working outside the home, therefore looking with sympathetic eyes at subjects such as widows, unmarried mothers and women incurring vast expenses to care for ill or disabled children. On the other hand, a second interpretation of Article 41.2.1-2 is that it perpetuates a most deplorable form of sexual stereotype. To begin with, it implies that life within the home is women's natural vocation. In addition, it refers to the duties of women as full-time wives and mothers while failing to mention or impose any duties on fathers.

Regrettably, Irish constitutional history appears to provide evidence that the second interpretation became the preferred option. Hence, Scannell (1988) shows that lawyers for the State attempted to justify tax discriminations against married women precisely on the basis of Article 41.2, and they succeeded in invoking the article to justify social welfare discriminations against deserted husbands obliged to take children into full-time care. For decades after the Constitution came into force, the position of women in Irish society remained virtually unchanged. In many cases, women were relegated to domesticity and powerlessness, while legislation based on the notion that their rights were somehow inferior to those of men made its appearance on the statute book. Notwithstanding the constitutional safeguards for marriage and motherhood, the *Oireachtas* seemed determined to keep women in the home by fair means or foul. As Scannell (1988, 127) forcefully argues,

> [c]ontraception was effectively illegal. The economically powerless home-maker was denied access to free legal aid. No financial aid was available as of rights to unmarried mothers, deserted wives or prisoners' wives, even when they were fulfilling their 'duties' in the home. The battered wife and mother could not exclude her violent husband from the home (which was almost invariably his) except by resort to the most cumbersome procedures. If she fled the home, her husband had a right to damages from anyone who enticed her away, or who harboured her or committed adultery with her.

Despite changing perceptions about the role of women in Irish society over the last thirty years, the debate over the at times uneasy relationship between Irish institutions and women is still ongoing.[2] To a certain extent,

---

[2] In recent years, for instance, debate has revolved around the issue of 'consent' following the notorious rugby rape trial. Cf. *The Guardian*. 2018. "How the 'rugby

this goes back to the controversy stirred by *Bunreacht na hÉireann* and its conceptualisation of female figures as worth a passive role in social intercourse (cf. Flynn 1998). In Chapter 4, we will see that women's status was a major issue in the conflicting opinions held by Irish newspapers on the Constitution upon its enactment.

1.6 *Bunreacht na hÉireann* and the Catholic Church

In many countries, the preservation of civic order also depends on earthly sanctions against transgressors. These may be reinforced by the strongly held belief that the law is sacred in character. As Mattila (2013, 57) accurately recalls, "Moses received the Commandments straight from the hand of God. In this set of beliefs, the administration of justice lay under the protection of the Most High. In consequence, contempt for the law and justice were considered" as a form of contempt for the Almighty himself. If the sacred character of the law has generally been reflected by both language and ritual, the way this has mobilised legal language and semiotics is closely correlated with each country's legal culture. One notable example is the solemn language of preambles to laws, where the legislator is acknowledged to have been empowered by no less than God.

The Irish State has been no exception to this trend. Indeed, there is no denying the influence of Catholic doctrine on the drafting of *Bunreacht na hÉireann*. This can be appreciated from a few well-known passages of the constitutional text, beginning with the Preamble itself. In particular, the opening lines read as follows (2018 [1937], 2):

> In the Name of the **Most Holy Trinity, from Whom is all authority and to Whom**, as our final end, all actions both of men and States must be referred,
>
> We, the people of Éire,
>
> Humbly acknowledging **all our obligations to our Divine Lord, Jesus Christ**, Who sustained our fathers through centuries of trial, […]
>
> Do hereby adopt, enact, and give to ourselves this Constitution. [My emphasis]

---

rape trial' divided Ireland". Accessed March 2, 2020. https://www.theguardian.com/news/2018/dec/04/rugby-rape-trial-ireland-belfast-case.

The notion that the Irish people recognise God's *authority* in relation to the law is by no means confined to the Preamble. In Article 6.1, accordingly, "all powers of government, legislative, executive and judicial" are said to "derive, under God, from the people" (2018 [1937], 8). Furthermore, Article 44.1 lays down that the "State acknowledges that the homage of public worship is due to Almighty God", "it shall hold his name in reverence" and "respect and honour religion" (2018 [1937], 174). Those ready to dismiss the *Bunreacht* as having been dictated to de Valera by John Charles McQuaid, Catholic Primate of Ireland and later Archbishop of Dublin, should, however, think again.

True enough, the original version of Article 44 itself, amended though it was in January 1973, provided for the State's recognition of "the special position of the Catholic Church" (1937, 144). Nevertheless, this formulation was less proof of de Valera's subservience than the result of his mediation efforts. An earlier draft of the Article actually specified that "the Church of Christ is the Catholic Church" (Daly 2020). Cardinal MacRory, a prominent figure of the Irish Hierarchy, had objected that the "special position" was too tentative a step, while McQuaid thundered that it was manifestly inadequate. In an effort to break the deadlock, de Valera sent an emissary to Rome from where, to his genuine regret, the Pope declined to give his blessing. In fact, the Holy See clarified that anything other than a reference to the "one true Church of Christ" would be seen as amounting to heresy. Nonetheless, the Pope's eventual decision neither to approve nor to disapprove gave de Valera the bargaining leverage he sought to reassert an uncompromising stance on the matter. "Despite the protestations of MacRory and McQuaid", Daly (2020) continues, "de Valera would not yield from his 'special position', with papal neutrality enough to avoid a divisive pre-plebiscite intervention by the Catholic hierarchy".

Over the last few decades, Ireland has changed substantially. The advent of the Celtic Tiger, a period of unprecedented economic growth and material well-being between the mid-1990s and the late 2000s, has led to an increasingly secular society. Young and middle-aged people are not as religiously observant as previous generations, while the Catholic Church's credibility has been severely damaged following the revelation of child abuse by the Catholic clergy and the "system of physical and psychological terror that operated outside the official parameters of the State" (Smyth 2012, 134) epitomised by such institutions as Magdalene Laundries and Industrial Schools. What emerged from the ashes of the boom, moreover, is a more complex picture of Irish society, where the influx of immigrants from Eastern Europe has revived Irish Catholic congregations, Orthodox Christianity is significantly present and the Muslim community is also well represented.

Even though the influence of the Catholic Church has waned considerably, the fact remains that in some parts at least, the Constitution still reflects dominant Catholic thinking on Church-State relations before the Second Vatican Council. Devoting a section to the relationship between the *Bunreacht* and the input from Catholicism as the religion of the preponderant majority of the nation is sensible for a number of reasons. First of all, the debate on the inclusion of references to God has been robust at an EU level, too, since many discussed or even countenanced the possibility of including them in the text of a European Constitutional Treaty. Secondly, "even though the religious scene is greatly changed" over the past few decades, a large number of people "continues to profess Catholicism" in Ireland, and "Catholic Church leaders will no doubt have something to say about any changes that may be proposed" to the Constitution "in regard to religious provisions" (Hannon 2008, 465).

1.7 Language and/in *Bunreacht na hÉireann*

The issue of the language of *Bunreacht na hÉireann* may not have been as fiercely debated as those of the representation of women or the influence of religion, but it deserves a passing mention in the broad overview provided by this chapter. Whether in relation to legislation or the Constitution, the Republic of Ireland's linguistic profile is bound to have an impact on drafting practices. According to Article 8.1 of the Constitution, Irish "as the national language is the first official language", while Article 8.2 describes the status of English as that of a "second official language recognised by the State" (2018 [1937], 8).

Regardless of the actual undisputed primacy of English in the country, consequently, due account must be taken of the centrality of Irish for official purposes, if nothing else. Not only has the presence of Irish in the country's public life generated heated discussion in relation to legal disputes where the use of the language in judicial proceedings has come to fore (cf. Mazzi 2018), but the *Bunreacht* itself is available both in English and in Irish. More precisely, Article 25.5.4 provides that "in case of conflict between the texts of any copy of this constitution enrolled under this section, the text in the national language shall prevail" (2018 [1937], 82). Briefly, this means that the Irish version is the authoritative one.

It is noteworthy that the Irish text of the Constitution was in preparation at the same time as the document was being drafted. This looks like a marked departure from the usual translation process beginning from a definitive text. Addressing the *Dáil* on 14 June 1937, de Valera stressed that providing an Irish version of the new charter was of no secondary importance to him. What he intended to achieve, he added, was by no means a direct translation from the English version. The drafting in Irish, so was his intention, was to progress along with the English on a step-by-step basis right from the beginning, when the main ideas were being recorded in draft form. "I want to tell those who suggest that the Irish was only an afterthought, a mere translation of the English," he said (in Ó Cearúil 1999, 1), "that the Irish drafting process has gone on *pari passu* almost from the beginning, when the fundamental ideas that were accepted for the Constitution were being put in draft form".

Interestingly, the Irish text of the *Bunreacht* was not produced by *Rannóg an Aistriúcháin*, the Translation Section of the Houses of the *Oireachtas*. The original draft of the Irish text was prepared by a man named Mícheál Ó Gríobhtha. A native of Co. Clare, his parents would speak English to the children, but Irish was commonly heard both at home and in the neighbouring area. After a few years spent teaching, Ó Gríobhtha became a highly qualified Customs and Excise Officer, before moving to the Department of Education. In that context, he mainly worked for *An Gúm*, the section in charge of publishing Irish-language materials. His native background as well as his experience as a civil servant made him ideally suited for the job, and he was handpicked by de Valera for the purpose. By the time it was decided that an Irish version of the Constitution would be developed (October 1936), Ó Gríobhtha, aged 67, was entrusted with the laborious task.

Ó Gríobhtha was seconded from the Department of Education, and from a room in Government Buildings, he started working on the Irish draft of *Bunreacht na hÉireann*. By mid-November, he is reported to have made good progress and he was joined by Risteárd Ó Foghludha, whom the Department also seconded as an editor. The two then worked together until the *Dáil* approved of the draft Constitution as a document to be submitted to the people in a referendum. A vivid account of their working method is provided by Mac Giolla Choille (in Ó Cearúil 1999, 3), who writes that

> Mícheál first [wrote] the Irish text as a precise and exact translation of the legal wording of the English version; Risteárd [edited] Mícheál's work, section by section and word by word, to make it more legible as Irish prose, or to bring it closer to ordinary speech as far as possible, without diminishing the meaning of the original version as regards law. Risteárd had a very heavy hand as editor and Mícheál must have had the patience of

> a saint. After the editing on the first version, for example, the alterations were so numerous that Mícheál had to sit down and write out a clear copy with Risteárd's corrections inserted in it, before they could start on the second drafting. From then on draft followed on draft so that the two of them bequeathed us a large collection of drafts, some complete and some relating to specific articles. They had to make new drafts also according as the English versions, which were being drafted and improved simultaneously, were being changed.

The draft of an Irish-language version of the Constitution must have presented Ó Gríobhtha, Ó Foghludha and their successors with formidable challenges in at least four respects. First of all, the search of appropriate terminology is likely to have posed thorny problems. In fact, it was only some twenty years after the Constitution was enacted that the well-known glossary *Téarmaí Dlí* [legal terms][3] was published (1960 [1957]). Not only, however, was the glossary limited in scope, but its terms were not used consistently in translating English legal language into Irish, whether for Acts of the *Oireachtas* or the Constitution itself. Secondly, a serious dilemma must have been created by the use of appropriate terminology within the grammatical constraints of a language as radically different from English as Irish. As O'Rourke (2014, 287) persuasively shows,

> the appropriate legal terms exist but they are not always easy to find. The matter of how to use them within the current grammatical constraints presents much more intractable difficulties. Irish has to become self-explanatory as distinct from using English as a semantic crutch so that we can begin to understand the real grammatical structure of the language.

In order to provide corroborating evidence of the *intractable difficulties* he alludes to, O'Rourke (2014) focuses on cross-linguistic differences regarding the verbal system of the two languages. Thus, for instance, he shows that, depending on context, Irish may translate the same English tense with up to four different tense forms.

In third place, a more contemporary issue than those addressed by Ó Gríobhtha and Ó Foghludha concerns gender-proofing. Since the mid-nineties, it has been a requirement that Acts of the *Oireachtas* be gender-proofed. At its simplest, in the English version of the Acts, this involves

[3] Here as well as elsewhere, unless otherwise stated, the translation of Irish into English is mine and represents a literal translation for the sake of clarity and consistent with any point raised about Irish-English divergences. Translation was based on the Author's knowledge of Irish and double-checked through Ó Dónaill (1977). Wherever present, emphasis is mine.

replacing *he* and *his* with *he or she* and *his or her*, respectively. In the Irish version, *sé* [he] should be removed and substituted for with *sé nó sí* [he or she], while "the personal pronoun 'a' followed by lenition of the initial consonant of the noun (e.g. 'a cheart', 'his right') now has, in addition to that, 'nó a' followed by the noun with unlenited initial consonant (i.e. 'a cheart nó a ceart', 'his right or her right')" (Ó Cearúil 1999, 47). Gender-proofing warrants, however, careful scrutiny.

On the one hand, there are passages where the original Irish text requires no intervention whatsoever: in Article 34.6.1, therefore, the complex prepositional sequence *gan eagla gan claonadh, gan bá gan drochaigne chun duine ar bith* literally translates as "with neither fear nor inclination, with neither sympathy nor malevolence towards **any person**", and as such requires no gender-proofing compared to the English-language version, namely "without fear or favour, affection or ill-will towards **any man**" (2018 [1937], 140).

On the other hand, there are contexts where, while the English text posed no problem, as in Article 44.1–"The state acknowledges that the homage of public worship is due to Almighty God" (2018 [1937], 174)–the Irish text needed amending. In *Admhaíonn an Stát go bhfuil ag dul do Dhia na nUilechumhacht é a adhradh le hómós go poiblí,* thus, more elaborate gender-proofing was actually necessary and involved an alteration to sentence structure. Not only does the above formulation contain *é* [him], but a simple replacement of it with *é nó í* would have implied referring to God as "him or her", which might have sounded a little awkward.

A gender-proofed version of the English text of the Constitution, under the auspices of the All-Party *Oireachtas* Committee on the Constitution, was published in the First Progress Report of that Committee, in April 1997. To his credit as a leading authority on the Irish text of the *Bunreacht* cited later in this work as well, it was Micheál Ó Cearúil who prepared a gender-proofed version of the Irish text of the Constitution for the Committee that was officially approved by the Translation Section of the Houses of the *Oireachtas*.

Finally, updates to the Constitution in the form of successive amendments suggest that current drafters should ensure overall consistency between any new passage to be included in the *Bunreacht* and the latter's pre-existing language, as it were. This work is not immediately concerned with the subtlety of a cross-linguistic study of the Constitution. However, the corpus study of its language in Chapter 4 will show that the differences between the two versions may be more marked than expected for a text the

Irish version of which is still considered by some a mere translation from English, as is the case with language choices in the field of modality.

A number of controversial aspects of the Constitution, from its treatment of Irish women to religion and language, have now been discussed. In the last two sections of the chapter, the overall historical and cultural significance of the Constitution is appreciated (1.8), before the general organisation of the volume is outlined in 1.9.

1.8 *Bunreacht na hÉireann*: Historical and cultural significance

Terms such as "historical", and even more so "cultural significance" should be used with extreme care in relation to Ireland. The Emerald Isle's cultural background is far more complex than meets the (non-expert) eye. Thus, the cultural nationalism which, directly or in association with republicanism, may have had profound influence on twentieth-century Ireland, was not merely Gaelic (Flower 1947). Rather, the waves of invaders and settlers from the Normans (late twelfth century) onwards altered and marked the Island's cultural pattern in various ways. In the wake of the defeat of the Chieftains in the early seventeenth century and the subsequent decline of the Irish language and native culture, the pre-existing Irish, Gaelic and Norman identity became closely interrelated with a Roman Catholic religious affiliation. Aspects such as this one should be reckoned with and are crucial to our understanding of, to name but one example, the Constitution's Preamble.

From a historical point of view, the Constitution has often been criticised for the supposedly narrow-minded nationalism it was assumed to embed. In Section 1.3, we actually saw that the first part of the *Bunreacht* contained provisions voicing a Republican aspiration to exercise jurisdiction over the whole of Ireland's 32 counties. It cannot be denied, however, that the Constitution never enabled the *Oireachtas* to legislate for Northern Ireland until the time of Ireland's formal reunification, which in any case is to be pursued through peaceful methods only. The Constitution, Daly (2020) aptly illustrates it, never contained a mandate for Dublin to resolve partition by violence. Nor did it implicitly empower the IRA or any other organisation to achieve the goal.

From a legal point of view, the Constitution's proclivity to incorporate Catholic social teaching was vastly outweighed by the wide array of provisions conferring fundamental rights on individual citizens. Accordingly, there is a firm guarantee of equal treatment; the State has a duty to provide free primary education; the personal rights of citizens must be protected and vindicated by the State; due process and, as we pointed out earlier on, *habeas corpus* rights are guaranteed; elections must be held by secret ballot, and the rights of association, assembly and expression are safeguarded. As shall be clear from the analysis in Chapter 6, moreover, Irish courts are granted strong powers of judicial review. Not only may they pronounce against the constitutionality of proposed legislation, but the President serves as "the watchdog of the Constitution" (Barrington 1987, 117) in that s/he is entitled to refer bills to the Supreme Court for a binding judgment on whether they are repugnant to the *Bunreacht* in whole or in part. A thorough analysis of the Constitution, Daly (2020) argues, suggests that

> the entrenchment of the separation of powers, judicial review and fundamental rights makes it a paradigmatic liberal democratic charter. With its generous provisions, guarantees of fair play in the electoral process, a president positioned to put a brake on abuses of power and courts vested with a strong power of judicial review, the constitution resembles the document that might emerge from a conclave of academic experts today, never mind 1937.

Generous though this interpretation may be taken to be, it succeeds in capturing the essence of the Constitution's historical significance: it is indeed striking for a document as protective of citizens' rights as this to have emerged from a period tainted by anti-democratic ideas firmly entrenched in Catholic authoritarianism, corporatism and fascism (Keogh and McCarthy 2007). In order to appreciate this, it is enough to look at the paradox of the *Seanad*, as it were. We know from Section 1.2 that de Valera had abolished the upper Chamber, arguably in response to its hindering his efforts to dismantle the Anglo-Irish Treaty. However, rather than drafting a constitution that would allow him to tighten his own grip on the country, he gave his blessing to a charter that revived the *Seanad*, albeit in a different institutional framework altogether.

From a broader cultural perspective, *Bunreacht na hÉireann* has been defined as the outcome of the interplay between Republican and liberal democratic ideals in a Catholic context, as is testified to by the articles on personal rights and religion. According to McDonagh (1987, 199), this unique combination

> was a continuation of the earlier coalition of democracy and human freedoms, including religious freedom which O'Connell had inspired and which attracted some favourable European and some unfavourable British and Roman attention in the first half of the nineteenth century. Article 43 on private property was a product of a similar convergence of traditions:

the insistence of Locke and various successors on the connection between private property and freedom, the nineteenth-century struggle of the dispossessed Irish for property rights, particularly in land, and the developing Catholic emphasis on the right to private property in the face of socialist and communist manifestos.

1.9 Organisation of the volume

This chapter was aimed at introducing readers to the actual object of this research, namely the Irish Constitution. Not only was the *Bunreacht* set against its own historical background (Section 1.2), but a number of distinctive aspects of the document were examined (Section 1.3), from the contentious provisions on sovereignty to fundamental (and unenumerated) rights. Moreover, the chapter has focused on the elements of the constitutional text that have sparked more intense controversy since its introduction, from the canons of constitutional interpretation (Section 1.4) to the conceptualisation of women (1.5), the influence of Roman Catholicism (1.6) and language issues arising from the bilingual version of the text (1.7). Finally, the overall historical significance of the Constitution has been assessed in the light of Ireland's rich cultural heritage (1.8).

In Chapters 2 and 3, more food for thought is provided about how the investigation of the Constitution was carried out here. To begin with, Chapter 2 contextualises our study of *Bunreacht na hÉireann* in the light of a number of theoretical approaches the volume aims at integrating. From corpus linguistics to argumentation theory, from historical news analysis to the study of judicial argumentation, the key concepts contributed by the research traditions and methodologies on which the current work draws are explored in detail. This serves the purpose of bringing forward a proposal to both develop a research plan envisaging a quantitative and qualitative analysis, and identify the gaps in knowledge the book is intended to fill. In Chapter 3, then, the basis is provided for the presentation of findings later in the book. In the first place, the chapter lays down the criteria through which the materials for the analysis were chosen. As will be illustrated, the study is based on three corpora as collections of authentic texts on which the analysis was performed.

Accordingly, more details are provided about the rationale behind corpus design and the characteristics of the collected corpora. In particular, the choice of the sources of corpus texts is justified, and the decision to ground the analysis on the Constitution itself, news texts from the period of its enactment and Supreme Court judgments on judicial review is defended in relation to the research questions framed in Section 1.1. Furthermore, the main methodological issues of the investigation are addressed. The objective of this is to make explicit the stages at which the analysis was performed. In that regard, emphasis is laid on the three main directions taken by the study by means of the interpretation of corpus data offered in Chapters 4-6.

In Chapter 4, the text of *Bunreacht na hÉireann* will be treated as a corpus in its own right, and as such will be interrogated in an attempt to establish what regular patters of language use emerge from it as a small database. First of all, a preliminary overview of corpus findings is presented, and a list of the most frequent lexical fields along with the related word forms and clusters is provided. Subsequently, the main functions performed by the selected word forms in context are described. As is highlighted by the examples, these range from legislative empowerment to a definition of the duties and prerogatives of the key institutional stakeholders acting as the main figures in the polity envisaged by Ireland's constitutional charter.

In Chapter 5, a comparative analysis is conducted of the 1937 issues of two national newspapers (*Irish Independent* and *Irish Press*), in order to document how they reacted to the enactment of the *Bunreacht*, they presented it to the respective readership and they "argued" different visions of it by often entertaining a kind of critical discussion with each other. The focus is therefore on the use of rhetorical resources through which *Irish Independent* and *Irish Press* described and in many respects constructed the Constitution of Ireland. First of all, the editorial stance of the two newspapers is reviewed; secondly, the chapter discusses the way the contentious issue of women's rights touched on in Section 1.5 is dealt with from the columns of both publications.

If Chapter 5 investigates the relationship between the Constitution and Irish society at the level of public discourse represented by the press, Chapter 6 moves on to the impact of constitutional norms at a higher level, namely by looking at *Bunreacht na hÉireann* as the yardstick by which to assess the acceptability of Acts of the *Oireachtas*. In particular, the research examines the argumentative discourse in the fifteen judgments delivered by the Supreme Court under Article 26 of the Constitution. The chapter will therefore assess whether there is a degree of consistency in the argumentative strategy chosen by Irish Justices as they decide on the compatibility of Acts with the letter of the country's fundamental law. As is shown by corpus data, pragmatic argumentation lies at the heart of the Supreme

Court's discourse, and its variants as well as the patterns of complex argumentation these are embedded in are outlined.

Finally, Chapter 7 aims to evaluate the impact and assess the significance of the study of the *Bunreacht* in the Irish public sphere conducted in the volume. First of all, results are discussed with regard to the research questions introduced in 1.1 and more extensively phrased in Chapters 4-6. Secondly, the application of the methods and findings presented earlier is considered in relation to future research. The final discussion argues for the cross-fertilisation of corpus perspectives with inputs from the qualitative study of patterns of lexis and argument as vital elements in the Republic of Ireland's public discourse on the Nation's founding charter.

CHAPTER TWO

STUDYING *BUNREACHT NA HÉIREANN*: AN INTEGRATED APPROACH

2.1 Introduction: The challenges of legal drafting

Chapter 1 featured an introduction to the Constitution of Ireland, its historical background, legal infrastructure and relevance to Irish civic life. In this chapter, a key question is examined: how can *Bunreacht na hÉireann* be studied from a discourse perspective? The issue is of vital importance to this research and is dealt with in light of the relevant literature from a wide range of disciplinary angles. What is argued here is that the centrality of such a document as a fundamental law to a country's public sphere is best addressed by bringing different perspectives to the investigation and integrating a variety of approaches.

In modern statehood, power is best defined as word power. In democratic societies as we know them from EU Member States and beyond, a crucial category of power in written form is no doubt the law. Under democratic conditions, legal rules call on the understanding and loyalty of the citizenship as represented by the active members of a legal community. Democratic States therefore aim at achieving a situation where citizens consider law and justice to be their own. It is a desirable end that the law, along with judicial as well as administrative decisions, is respected by people of their own full accord, so that the legal community essentially acts as a community of persuasion. In order for this to work, it should be borne in mind that abiding by legal rules is inextricably linked to the content of the legal order, whereby unjust laws are not adhered to by citizens. At the same time, the appearance of laws plays an important role. In this respect, the appropriate choice of words and style encourages citizens to commit themselves to law and justice.

Within the broad category of legal writing, drafting "is concerned with preparing texts which are drawn up to be legally binding by establishing sets of rules or laws designed to govern or regulate the conduct of a given group of individuals or community" (Williams 2018, 15). As opposed to legal analysis, which includes law-related documents such as memoranda, letters to clients, and more persuasive forms of communication instantiated by appellate briefs or negotiation letters written on clients' behalf in their defence, European legal drafting is embedded in a time-honoured tradition. To a large extent, this developed in the ecclesiastical, royal, feudal and municipal chanceries and law courts of the Middle Ages, where the so-called "chancery style" came to life. Well-known features of legal documents, e.g. a high lexical density, the sheer complexity of sentences and the enduring attachment to ritual features and archaic forms, tend to originate from this style (Mellinkoff 1963; Tiersma 2012).

It follows that, despite reactions to the overall difficulty of accessing legal documents on laypeople's part, legal drafting appears to involve a highly formal and complex writing style. This was refined over the centuries, as the need to achieve extreme precision and detail was increasingly felt in response to constant pressure to produce texts standing up to scrutiny from lawyers and judges. Balancing the demand for precision, however, has always been a search for flexibility, in the hope that legal texts would be well suited to the different kinds of situation that may arise. Hence the reiterated use of both terms of art with very specific meaning and seemingly vague words such as *reasonable*, *reckless*, *prompt* or *fair*.

Achieving an optimum balance between the need for precision and flexibility is a daunting task. This may explain why legal, and in particular legislative drafting, is carried out as a collaborative activity in which several people–including, but not limited to, elected representatives such as local councillors and politicians with little (if any) legal training–"contribute, to varying degrees, to the final draft of the text, whereas the number of people involved in drafting a contract is usually very small" (Williams 2018, 18). Moreover, the duties and professional expertise of legislative drafters vary depending on country, organisation and, in particular, legal culture or tradition.

In the United Kingdom, for much of Government primary legislation, drafting is a prerogative of the Office of Parliamentary Counsel (OPC), which is formally within the Cabinet Office. The OPC also takes charge of drafting government amendments to legislation introduced during the parliamentary process. In addition, when instructed to do so, the OPC drafts some secondary legislation and reviews legislation intended to amend primary legislation, in order to ensure consistency. However, the division between the formulation of policy and the drafting of implementing legislation should not be overemphasised. In fact, once the instructions have been received, close liaison is established between the instructing ministry and the lawyers in the OPC drafting the legislation, with the ministerial committee supervising draft Government legislation and, once the draft legislation is introduced into Parliament, with officials of the Parliament itself addressing procedural matters (Bates 2009, 4).

In the Republic of Ireland, the country on which the book centres, the process that culminates in Government and Private Members' Bills (PMBs) is fairly complex. With PMBs, on the one hand, TDs and Senators that are not in government undertake their own research on the policy proposals underlying their proposed legislation. The Office of the Parliamentary Legal Advisers (OPLA) serves to assist them in exploring the legal issues arising from their policy proposals and helps with the drafting of the bill.[1]

In the case of Government Bills, a Minister intending to bring forward legislation must, in accordance with requirements set out in the Cabinet Handbook, obtain a Government decision authorising the drafting of that legislation. After a decision is obtained, the Minister requests the Attorney General to arrange for the drafting of a bill. The request is then passed on to the Group Manager in the Office of Parliamentary Counsel, where requests from the Minister's Department are dealt with. Subsequently, the Group Manager entrusts a Parliamentary Counsel with the task of drafting the bill. The function of Parliamentary Counsel is to transpose the policy of the Department into a draft bill in clear and precise terms.

During the drafting process, legal issues of various kinds may arise. These may lead Parliamentary Counsel to turn to another lawyer, known as an Advisory Counsel, for advice. Parliamentary Counsel may occasionally have to consult with the Attorney General during the drafting process. When the relevant legal as well as policy issues have been settled, the Department and the Office go through the draft. If they are satisfied with it, the Parliamentary Counsel assigned to draft the Bill transmits the final version to the Department. The Minister will then present the Bill to Cabinet for a decision to publish the Bill. Parliamentary Counsel also drafts all Government amendments moved at Committee or Report Stage as the bill passes through the Houses of the *Oireachtas*.[2]

The delicate handling of and serious challenges posed by legal drafting also confront constitution drafters. In fact, these must be faced with genuine linguistic dilemmas as constitutions "contain declarations that

[1] Houses of the *Oireachtas*. N.d. "How laws are made". Accessed January 13, 2020. https://www.oireachtas.ie/en/visit-and-learn/how-parliament-works/how-laws-are-made/.

[2] Office of the Attorney General. N.d. "What Parliamentary Counsel do". Accessed February 12, 2020. http://www.attorneygeneral.ie/pc/pc_do.html.

relate to the fundamental values of society. Examples include the right of citizens to obtain work and enough to live on"; furthermore, since "one classic value of particular importance declared by Constitutions is equality of citizens" (Mattila 2013, 52), drafters need to be deeply sensitive to language subtleties encoded in a document meant to regulate a country's society and institutions for a long time to come. Rather than dealing with the Irish Constitution from the point of view of drafters or legal practitioners, however, this work explores the complexity of *Bunreacht na hÉireann* from a discourse perspective.

In order to assess the significance of this historical document, in particular, the research begins by analysing the language of the *Bunreacht* through the lens of corpus linguistics (Chapter 4). In Section 2.2, accordingly, the essential features of this methodological framework are pointed out. In addition, the volume evaluates the impact of the Constitution on Irish public discourse at two main levels. First of all (Chapter 5), the study focuses on the way two prominent national media outlets received the news of the draft and subsequent enactment of the charter. By looking at news stories, letters to the editor and editorials from 1937, therefore, the analysis sheds light on the way(s) the Constitution was represented and "argued" from different viewpoints. On the basis of a collection of Article 26 judgments, secondly (Chapter 6), the focus shifts from popular to specialised discourse, in order to account for the main strategies through which Supreme Court Justices pronounce on the constitutionality of bills.

A common trait of Chapters 5 and 6 is the analysis of argumentative discourse as it emerges from both news and judicial texts. Hence, Section 2.3 illustrates the core concepts from argumentation theory relevant to the investigation. In Section 2.4, then, a brief overview of the role of news media in Irish society after Independence is provided, before Section 2.5 moves on to the domain of judicial argumentation. To begin with, Subsections 2.5.1 and 2.5.2 briefly discuss the issue of the justification of judicial decisions in legal settings and in argumentation studies, respectively. Finally, key aspects of legal interpretation in the Republic of Ireland are considered in Subsection 2.5.3.

2.2 Corpus linguistics: A brief overview

A corpus (plural *corpora*) can be defined as a collection of texts gathered for a particular reason and based on a set of uniform criteria (Cheng 2012). Random collections of texts do not therefore qualify as corpora, while a primary criterion behind corpus compilation is usually the attempt to ensure that corpora are representative of a particular register, genre or variety of language. Not surprisingly, among the major issues concerning corpus design are those of corpus size and type.

Arguably, the ideal size for a corpus–from a few thousand to more than a million words–depends on the investigation pursued by analysts, e.g. grammar as opposed to lexicography studies. In any case, the view that the bigger the corpus, the better, should be qualified. Thus, Stubbs (1996, 81-100) performed a comparative analysis of two speeches by Baden-Powell which, taken together, amounted to less than 1,000 words. Despite the seemingly limited amount of data, the author managed to observe noticeable differences in usage between the two speeches by using corpus tools effectively.

As regards the type of corpora to be collected for analysis, a fundamental distinction should be drawn between diachronic and synchronic corpora. The former are "built in order to be representative of a language or language variety over a particular period of time, so that it is possible for researchers to track linguistic changes within" them, whereas synchronic corpora focus on texts that cover a more limited and homogeneous time span (Baker et al. 2006, 56). Furthermore, the need to design more reliable corpora underlies the analyst's choice of either general or specialised corpora. General corpora, such as the British National Corpus (*BNC*) or the International Corpus of English–Ireland (*ICE_Ireland*) "provide the means for studying how English is used in general contexts" such as service encounters of various sorts or the press, "while the development of specialised corpora provide[s] the means for studying how English is used in special contexts" including the domains of business or the law (Noguchi et al. 2006, 156).

As the scholarly enterprise devoted to the compilation and analysis of corpora, corpus linguistics refers to the set of studies into the form and/or function of language undertaken by interrogating corpora. As such, it can be seen as a form of text linguistics and it is inherently evidence-driven. More specifically, McEnery and Wilson (1996, 1) argue that it is the "study of language based on examples of 'real life' language use" and a "methodology rather than an aspect of language requiring explanation or description". Indeed, most corpus linguists agree that corpus texts should be naturally-occurring, i.e. written or spoken in real-world contexts. The reason behind this preference is that they strive to account for regularities in language and propose theories that are by definition grounded in actual language use. As a result, "they see no benefit in examining invented texts or texts that have been manipulated by the researcher" (Cheng 2012, 4).

As an increasingly sophisticated combination of tools and techniques for linguistic analysis, corpus linguistics can be accounted for as a methodological paradigm, "where paradigm means analytical model of the part of the universe under analysis, here, language structure and use" (Partington et al. 2013, 7). One of the main advantages of corpus linguistics is that it provides better quality evidence, because it enables one to scientifically establish the regularity of patterns owing to their repetition across corpus texts. Conversely, single, isolated instances of language use, however authentic, do not allow for such a systematic analysis of language in the absence of the multiple instances retrieved through large corpora. Intuitive though it is to conceive of corpus linguistics as an inherently quantitative paradigm, the term *quantitative* itself deserves further elucidation.

By "quantitative", we mean that most of the linguistic analysis conducted through corpora avails itself of statistical evidence, grounded as it so often is on computerised methods. In its search and overriding concern for recurring patterns, corpus linguistics embraces the twin concepts of frequency as a factor of past observation, and probability as a factor of future predictability. If, in other words, something is identified as occurring frequently, then it is significant. Its significance lies in the fact that its regularity may serve as a basis to predict how other yet unaccounted for chunks of language will behave, and eventually to formulate plausible hypotheses on how larger segments of the discourse under investigation are altogether constructed. Moreover, while the early stages of corpus analysis are generally quantitative, the patterns established through corpus techniques require interpretation. This may involve a second stage of analysis where the linguistic software packages are first used as an aid to analysts in surveying linguistic data more rapidly. As the research moves apace, however, "the analysis gradually becomes more qualitative and context-led, relying less on computer software" (Baker and McEnery 2015, 2).

In approaching corpus data, analysts generally carry out corpus-based or corpus-driven investigations. The former "use[s] a corpus as a source of examples to check researcher intuition or to examine the frequency and/or plausibility of the language contained within a smaller data set" (Baker et al. 2006, 49). In corpus-based studies, analysis do not intend to question traditional descriptive units and categories. In this, their approach is deductive because their reasoning moves from the more general to the more specific in what Tognini Bonelli (2001, 10-11) sees as a "top-down approach".

On the other hand, corpus-driven projects are those where corpora themselves are the data and the patterns in them are noted as a way of expressing regularities as well as exceptions in language. As a rule, corpus-driven studies only use theoretical presuppositions about grammatical structure sparingly. The corpus-driven approach is thus inductive: by proceeding from specific observations to broader generalisations and theories, it works as a bottom-up approach. Analysts begin from specific observations and measures in their quest for patterns and regularities. When patterns have been identified, they put forward tentative hypotheses worth exploring and, at best, developing into some general conclusions (Tognini Bonelli 2001, 14-18).

But what do corpus linguists look at in the corpora they have compiled? Essentially, they are interested in "lexical items", which Sinclair (2004, 141-142) described as comprised of up to five categories of co-selection, notably the core, collocation, colligation, semantic preference and semantic prosody. The first is the "core", namely "the word or words, always present in every instance of a lexical item" (Cheng 2012, 114). Next is "collocation", that is "how a particular word or expression co-occurs with other words or sequences of words with particular frequency" (Partington et al. 2013, 18).

It is a fact that native speakers of a language draw on a repertoire of thousands of collocates stored in their memories, so that hearing or reading one word is likely to prime another. However, collocational patterns are hardly available to unassisted introspection on a large scale, which leads one to appreciate the valuable role of corpora in linguistic observation. The large-scale implementation of collocational analysis is key to retrieving "clusters". These are multi-word units, i.e. sequences or strings of words that "are found repeatedly together in each other's company" (Scott 2010, 337). Such phrases are variously termed "bundles" (Biber et al. 1999), "formulaic expressions" (Wray 2002) or "n-grams". Although these terms are treated as synonyms in this volume, there will be a definite preference for "clusters" as defined earlier on, and "n-grams", where *n* indicates the number of words in the sequence, so that a 4-gram is a four-word chunk.

Clusters or n-grams have warranted serious scholarly attention as they are a prime example of phraseology as the tendency of words to go together and make meaning by virtue of their combination. Not only do they "have identifiable discourse functions, suggesting that they are important for the production and comprehension of texts" (Biber 2006, 155), but they have also been associated with major aspects of specialised texts. Accordingly, the adoption of corpus-driven methods and multidimensional analysis pointed to their frequency as evidence of their operative function in communicating key procedural aspects of judicial decisions (Gozdz-Roszkowski 2011; Pontrandolfo 2013).

The third category is "colligation", which relates to "the co-selection of grammatical choices with the core" (Cheng 2012, 114). Finally, "semantic preference" is "the relation, not between individual words, but between a lemma or word-form and a set of semantically-related words" (Stubbs 2001, 65), while "semantic (or discourse) prosody" describes "the way that words in a corpus can collocate with a related set of words or phrases, often revealing (hidden) attitudes" (Baker et al. 2006, 58). Thus, Sinclair (1991) demonstrated that the verb phrase *set in* carries a negative prosody by reason of its tendency to collocate with items such as the noun *rot*. Interestingly, no obvious negative connotation is attached to *set in*, which therefore derives its prosody from its surrounding co-text, possibly because people unconsciously remember the context in which they heard the phrase in the past and tend to use it themselves in similarly negative ways.

From a practical point of view, one way to detect patterns of use and co-selection is by looking at the most frequent word forms across corpus frequency lists, n-gram lists and keyword lists. Whereas the first two respectively arrange word forms and n-grams (whatever the required length set by the analyst at the outset, e.g. 4-6-grams), keyword lists involve carrying out a comparative survey, so to speak. At their simplest, keywords are those word forms that are signalled by a corpus software as more frequent than expected in one corpus, when set against a second, usually larger, reference corpus typically assumed to be representative of the relevant standard language. Keywords "reveal words which may not be hugely frequent but are definitely statistically salient in some way" (Baker and McEnery 2015, 2). Word forms that appear to be prominent in frequency lists, at the core of n-grams and even in keyword lists may be those worth studying in more detail, mostly through concordances.

Also known as key words in context, concordances are lists of all the occurrences of a search term (or phrase) in a corpus, displayed "in its own textual environment" (Sinclair 1991, 32)–typically a few words to the left and right of it. Concordances are an extremely handy tool because they "can usually be sorted alphabetically on either the search term itself or to x places left or right of the search term, allowing linguistic patterns to be more easily observed by humans" (Baker et al. 2006, 43). Sorting concordances facilitates human interpretation particularly when a word or phrase occurs hundreds or thousands of times. When this happens, it is desirable to look at smaller samples of concordance lines: once these have been sorted, patterns will become more easily noticeable in that "the software will randomly reduce or 'thin' the number of lines to a more manageable amount" (Baker and McEnery 2015, 3).

The corpus analytic tools reviewed above, from keywords to concordance lines, have been developed by scholars in research pulling in different directions. One is to triangulate methodological approaches. In Baker and Egbert (2016), the authors of the chapters collected in the book were asked to apply different methods (e.g., keywords, lexical bundles, collocation and many others) to the same data set. In order to stimulate careful reflection on the opportunity to integrate various analytical tools to glean a higher degree of insight, the two editors then review the methods used in the study in terms of their strengths and limitations. Thus, for instance, they acknowledge that keyword analysis can be described as a useful method to compare corpora for the purpose of discovering what makes them distinctive or similar. Nonetheless, they also emphasise "the need for contextualization and interpretation–in the form of close reading of concordance lines and investigating collocations–both of which require sufficient data to support conclusions" (Egbert and Baker 2016, 196).

A further direction taken by corpus studies in recent years is represented by corpus-assisted discourse studies (CADS). As a subset of corpus linguistics proper, CADS is conceptualised by Partington et al. (2013, 10) as "that set of studies into the form and/or function of language as *communicative discourse* which incorporate the use of computerised corpora in their analyses". When CADS was born, its underlying notion was that of an eclectic approach, where corpus techniques enable analysts to generate only part of the findings, and observation also comes from other sources of information outside corpora themselves. Hence the term "corpus-assisted" to qualify "discourse studies". CADS is intended to approach a discourse type and uncover non-obvious meaning. On the assumption that much of what carries meaning in text is not immediately open to direct observation, CADS analysts set out to combine statistical overviews of large amounts of data with the more inherently qualitative approach of discourse analysis.

In corpus linguistics proper, researchers are not always encouraged to go through even a subset of corpus texts, in order to avert the danger that the features characterising them may end up impairing their sound judgment about the corpus as a whole. In this respect, the idea is that the attempt to develop descriptive models of language relying on naturally-occurring discourse as much as possible requires one to trust the text and let the data speak for themselves (Sinclair 2004, 185-186). Conversely, CADS invites analysts to familiarise themselves thoroughly with the discourse type they are investigating. The more they engage with the data they work with, so the argument runs, the more accurate their assessment of data is going to be. Along with frequency lists and concordances, therefore, they are encouraged to trust intuition arising "from reading or watching or listening to parts of the data-set, a process which can help provide a feel for how things are done linguistically in the discourse-type being studied" (Partington et al. 2013, 12).

In this work, Chapter 5 is the most widely corpus-linguistic, as it were. Unlike in most studies, however, where corpora include many a text, here the Irish Constitution itself is treated as a synchronic, specialised corpus in its own right. In order to examine the discourse of the *Bunreacht* as rigorously as its size affords, a corpus-driven approach is adopted. Once the salient lexical items have been extracted (see Chapter 3), the preferred tool is the concordance, which is used to detect the most common collocational surroundings of the selected word forms and account for their discourse function in context. By following one of the basic tenets of CADS, moreover, the interpretation of linguistic patterns is always supported by the analyst's familiarity with both the corpus itself and the context in which it was produced, as it was established in Chapter 1. In Chapters 5 and 6, two corpora are actually used. It is fair to say, however, that the investigation of both is less corpus-linguistic than discourse analytic. Although linguistic regularity is not discarded (most notably in Chapter 5), the study is more narrowly focused on the identification of pervasive argument schemes informing the representation of the Constitution in the Irish press, and the interpretation of proposed legislation in light of the *Bunreacht* by Supreme Court Justices. As a cornerstone of Chapters 5 and 6, the study of argumentation is a central issue of the next section.

2.3 Argumentation studies: Key notions

The notion and fundamental principles of argumentation have been dealt with for centuries. For it is beyond the scope of this work to trace its roots in the context of the long-established tradition of ancient rhetoric,[3] the definition of "argumentation" presented here originates from the dominant paradigms of present-day argumentation theory.

The leading Dutch theorist Frans Van Eemeren (2001, 11) sees argumentation as "a verbal, social and rational activity aimed at convincing

[3] For an overview of the historical development of argumentation studies from ancient rhetoric to the present day, see Mazzi (2007).

a reasonable critic of the acceptability of a standpoint by advancing a constellation of propositions justifying or refuting the proposition expressed in the standpoint". The merits of this comprehensive vision are apparent. First of all, argumentation is conceived of as "verbal": this shows that there is an inherent linguistic dimension to reasoning processes. Secondly, argumentation is "social" and "rational": this rightly suggests that argumentation is both an activity presupposing reason ("rational") and one that unfolds in contexts of interaction ("social"), whether it be face-to-face discussions or more mediated communication between one or more writers and their prospective readership. Thirdly, the aim of argumentation is to get the interlocutor (or reader) involved to accept the speaker's (or writer's) standpoint: the addressees of argumentation are called "reasonable critics" because they are both entitled to question–let alone reject–a standpoint (hence the term "critic"), and expected to operate in a way that is appropriate in view of the communicative and interactional situation ("reasonable").

By definition, therefore, argumentation is put forward as a response to, or in anticipation of, a difference of opinion. In its capacity as a framework to regulate disagreement, argumentation is devoted to resolving a difference of opinion by providing a justification–or refutation–of the standpoint under discussion, thereby dispelling doubts about the acceptability of such standpoint. The need for argumentation, its structure as well as the requirements that it should meet under scrutiny, are related to the doubts or criticisms that must be addressed by means of arguing. In pragma-dialectics, argumentative discourse is seen as a purposive verbal activity whose structure is essentially determined by this function.

For the purpose of clarifying the implications of a notion of argumentative discourse as geared to resolve differences of opinion on the merits, pragma-dialecticians developed an ideal model of critical discussion. Ideally, the parties involved in the discussion strive to reach agreement on the acceptability of the standpoint at issue. They therefore engage with one another by finding out whether the standpoint holds against critical doubt in light of certain mutually accepted starting points. In this context, pragma-dialectics specifies the stages to be distinguished in the resolution process as well as the speech acts underpinning the argumentative moves instrumental at each stage. One outstanding merit of the approach has been to give context its rightful place in the study of argumentation.

By forging a close connection between the theory and argumentative reality, the contextual dimension of the communicative activity types of domains such as the legal, political, medical and academic was incorporated in the theorisation (Van Eemeren 2010 and 2011). During argumentative exchanges, participants are thus assumed to take the institutional preconditions of the communicative type and the relevant critical reactions into account, when a certain argument scheme is being advanced. “Argument schemes” are forms of reasoning that create “a specific justifying relationship between the applied argument or […] the applied arguments and the standpoint at issue” (Van Eemeren et al. 2007, 137). Depending on the kind of justifying relationship the argumentation is based on, three main types of argumentation are identified. Each one of these has its own argument scheme, namely argumentation by comparison, symptomatic argumentation and causal argumentation.

As is shown in Chapters 5 and 6, the most widely used schemes in the corpora under investigation here are symptomatic and causal argumentation. While the latter appears crucial to judicial reasoning and is therefore discussed in Section 2.5 (Subsection 2.5.2), symptomatic argumentation can be introduced in the current section. In argumentation resting on a symptomatic relationship, “a property, class membership, distinctive characteristic, or essence of a particular thing, person, or situation referred to in the argumentation also applies to the thing, person or situation referred to in the standpoint” (Van Eemeren et al. 2007, 154). Symptomatic argumentation is associated by pragma-dialecticians to the following schematisation:

> Y is true of X
> because Z is true of X
> and Z goes characteristically together with Y

The scheme is observed by Van Eemeren et al. (2007) to apply to examples such as the following: “Bill is very egocentric because he is an only child”. In this sentence, the fact that Bill belongs to the set of people who are an only child is used to support the conclusion that he also displays the characteristic of being egocentric that typically goes with this class. Such a symptomatic relation also works in the opposite direction. The fact that Bill is egocentric is then used as an argument justifying the conclusion that he must be an only child: “Bill must be an only child because he is egocentric and egocentrism is characteristic of people who are an only child”.

The use of argument schemes of this kind results in the creation of what Van Eemeren (2016, 14) calls “argumentative patterns” in the discourse, that is sets of “argumentative moves in which, in order to deal with a particular kind of difference of opinion, in defence of a particular type of standpoint a particular argument scheme or combination of argument schemes is used in a particular kind of argumentation structure”. In turn, the reconstruction of schemes and patterns leads to uncover the structure of argumentative discourse, notably the overall articulation of schemes into multiple or coordinative argumentation supporting the standpoint.

It is noteworthy that pragma-dialecticians are interested in evaluating argumentative discussions or texts, in order to determine “whether the argument schemes that the defender of a particular standpoint uses are in fact appropriate and correctly applied” (Van Eemeren et al. 2007, 137). In this work, by contrast, the approach is primarily descriptive rather than normative: the emphasis is on the retrieval of the main argument schemes through which newspapers represent and “argue” the Constitution (Chapter 5), and Supreme Court Justices assess the constitutionality of bills submitted to them by the Irish President (Chapter 6). The aim of the analysis is therefore less to evaluate the appropriateness of the argumentation than to reconstruct the prototypical schemes and patterns at the core of Irish public discourse on *Bunreacht na hÉireann* in 1937 and over the last decades. News and judicial discourse being the focus of Chapters 5 and 6, they are respectively discussed in relation to Ireland in the two sections that follow.

2.4 Setting the scene: The news media in post-Independence Ireland

Journalism in Ireland experienced an unprecedented expansion at the turn of the twentieth century as a result of such factors as the introduction of a national system of education (1831) and increased literacy rates (Tobin 2018), the abolition of stamp duty, improved operational efficiency paired with decreasing costs of resources, tools and processes, cheaper transport for distribution and higher population concentrations due to urbanisation (Morash 2010). Irish journalism thus came of age during a time of momentous change and against a background of cultural ferment and ever-increasing political agitation in the build-up to the Easter Rising (1916) and the War of Independence (1919-1921) (Rafter 2011; Mazzi 2019). The gradual development of a civil society between the last decades of the nineteenth century and the late 1910s was to have far-reaching implications for the development of Irish politics. As Kissane (2002, 113) rightly points out,

> If civil society is a sphere in which democratic practices can develop, in which an autonomous public opinion can be formed, and in which people

acquire the skills that make them effective citizens in a modern polity, then the development of Irish civil society should be regarded as a precondition of the emergence of Irish democracy between 1918 and 1922.

Well into the twentieth century, journalists could be said to work within and "contribute to an embryonic public sphere and a growing civil society, which led to a democratic culture that was influenced by an increased civic involvement in Britain, the Continent and in Ireland itself" (Foley 2004, 383).

After Independence (1922), Irish public life and media were to be profoundly shaped by the severe historical trauma of the Civil War. The war erupted as a result of the Anglo-Irish Treaty signed in December 1921. Among the terms and conditions of the Treaty were an oath of allegiance to the British Monarch Irish Members of Parliament (TDs) were supposed to take before taking office, and the right of Northern Ireland to opt out and remain part of the United Kingdom, thereby paving the way to Partition (Fitzpatrick 1992). Although the Treaty was ratified by *Dáil Éireann* and carried by popular vote, which underpinned the establishment of the Irish Free State, doctrinaire Republicans split away and refused to accept it, leading to a war that was to rage between June 1922 and May 1923. As Ferriter (2005, 264) shows, the increasing barbarity of both Free Staters and Republicans was symbolised by two appalling atrocities: after a mine claimed the lives of five Free State soldiers at Knocknagoshel in County Kerry, "in reprisal eight republicans were tied to a mine and blown up at Ballyseedy, Tralee, also in Kerry. According to Dorothy Macardle, for days after 'the birds were eating the flesh off the trees at Ballyseedy Cross'".

In the Civil War period, media outlets such as the *Republic of Ireland* and the *Catholic Bulletin* championed de Valera, the most prominent political figure behind the Republican split, after the signing of the Treaty. The *Republic of Ireland* endorsed de Valera's ambition to receive international recognition for an Irish Republic, despite the Treaty. Even though it eventually supported the Government's appeal to the Irish people to view the English as the only enemy, it had notoriously defended de Valera even after he delivered such divisive speeches apparently preaching civil war as in Killarney on 18 March 1922, when he said that

> in future, in order to achieve freedom, if our Volunteers continue, and I hope they will continue until the goal is reached–if we continue on that movement which was begun when the Volunteers were started, and we suppose this Treaty is ratified by your votes, then these men, in order to achieve freedom, will have, I said yesterday, to march over the dead bodies

> of their own brothers. They will have to wade through Irish blood. (de Valera in Moynihan 1980, 103).

The *Catholic Bulletin*, which had praised the men who joined the Easter Rising, upheld de Valera's decision not to participate in the Treaty negotiations and accused the Irish delegation of failing to follow his instructions properly. Increasingly partisan as it became, the *Bulletin* invited its readers to consider de Valera's proposals as a viable alternative to the Treaty, and assured them that the British Government would be ready to negotiate further, if the Irish people stood united behind de Valera.

On the other side of the political divide, the *Freeman's Journal* conveyed the unmistakable message that the Free State's Provisional Government ought to be supported. It called for full implementation of the Treaty and the rebuilding of the Irish economy, which had contracted dramatically during the War of Independence. It took a firm stand against de Valera, whom it accused of dividing the nation, and it described Republicans as disruptive of law and order in the country. A weekly publication, the *Free State* also favoured the Treaty. With people such as Desmond Fitzgerald and Eoin MacNeill on board, the paper was intended to oppose the anti-Treaty narrative constructed by organs such as the *Republic of Ireland*, and it insisted that the Irish people only would have a right to decide whether the Treaty secured a satisfactory settlement of the Irish question.

A most comprehensive account of the poisoned atmosphere prevailing in the Irish media landscape at the time is offered by Glandon (1985, 225), who points out that, during the summer of 1922,

> the *Free State* and the *Republic of Ireland* expressed even more widely divergent views. The first named paper urged all the Irish people to reconcile their differences through the constitutional process, while the last named paper appeared to condone the use of bullets, if Irish Republicans could achieve their goals no other way. Each paper published its share of petty, satirical remarks and poetry about those who opposed its particular point of view, as Ireland moved toward civil war.

In an attempt to change the prevailing ideological climate fostered by the Civil War, even *Truth*, until then a periodical containing little else than Free State propaganda, went to great lengths to persuade the Irish people to stand by their elected government and transcend bitter divisions. It solicited full support for the Free State Army as the only body to be trusted with the restoration of democracy and the end of the rule of gun. In doing so, it sought to enlist workers' support, too, and along with most other 26-county newspapers, it "urged the settlement of political differences and an end to the war" (Glandon 1985, 229).

The end of the Civil War eased an orderly transition to democracy, where even such Republican hardliners as de Valera would be gradually absorbed by democratic processes. In this context, a watershed moment in the years after the war was precisely the adoption of a new Constitution, a document conceived to stabilise the country by designing a system of checks and balances for State institutions, asserting fundamental rights and articulating directive principles of social policy. The context of 1930s Ireland that formed the background to the enactment of *Bunreacht na hÉireann* confirmed the significant presence of the *Irish Independent* among the country's best selling newspapers, while it heralded the emergence of new publications such as the *Irish Press*, a rising star in the country's news discourse. In Chapter 5, the role of these two newspapers is further elucidated, before their stance towards the Constitution is taken into consideration.

2.5 Judicial argumentation at a glance

2.5.1 The justification of judicial decisions in legal theory

In States based on democratic accountability enhanced by checks and balances, courts are expected to both settle disputes and justify their decisions. As they outline the reasons underlying their verdict, judges advance argumentation. By doing so, they address a multi-faceted audience including the parties and their legal representatives, fellow judges as well as courts higher up in the judicial hierarchy, for the purpose of showing them that their decision was made on legitimate grounds. In the law, Perelman (1978, 1979 and 1980) argued, no power can be exercised arbitrarily. Whether in the case of measures introduced by public authorities or in that of the adjudicating power of courts, more specifically, the law entails both an act of authority and one of reasoning in the context of the existing legal order.

In the field of legal theory, a wide range of scholars have focused on the peculiarity of the distinctive aspects that guide accepted interpretative practices and inform judicial argumentation. For instance, Alexy (1989 [1978]) examined some of the characteristics inherent in legal systems, from the vagueness of legal language to the likelihood of conflicting norms, from the recurrence of hard cases to decisions that appear to be contrary to the wording of statutes themselves. His comprehensive account of such features raises the issue of how judgments can be rationally justified in the complex network of constraints imposed by the law. Similarly, Aarnio (1989) also emphasised the role of justification in judicial decision making. In the attempt to develop a repertoire of methods of judicial interpretation, he began by distinguishing authoritative and substantial legal reasons. On the one hand, the former are articulated by sources such as statutes, *travaux préparatoires* and court rulings. On the other hand, substantial legal reasons acquire significance due to their relevance to specific cases, as with general legal or moral principles and the custom of the land. He then provided an overview of reasoning procedures followed by courts: standards of grammatical interpretation, extensive and restrictive interpretations, *argumentum a fortiori*, principles of analogy and conclusions *e contrario*.

2.5.2 The justification of judicial decisions in argumentation studies

From the perspective of mainstream argumentation theory, the issue of how to justify judicial decisions has been addressed by pragma-dialecticians, who examine argument structure in the resolution of differences of opinion on the merits. More specifically, a number of studies have elucidated the role of pragmatic argumentation in judicial decision-making (Feteris 2002, Bustamante 2013 and Carbonell 2013). By definition, pragmatic argumentation is consequentialist argumentation in that "judges often defend a decision by referring to the consequences of application of a particular legal rule in the concrete case" (Feteris 2002, 349). Interestingly, Feteris distinguishes two main variants: a positive variant, whereby the acceptability of an act, decision or interpretation is defended by envisaging its positive future consequences; and a negative variant, in which conversely the unacceptability of the act is argued to derive from the negative effects it would produce.

Overall, pragmatic argumentation can be seen as a subtype of causal argumentation (Van Eemeren et al. 2007, 166), which is known to have been investigated in many a work over the past centuries. For instance, the existence of causal links drew the attention of thinkers such as John Locke. In Book II (Chapter XXVI) of his *Treatise concerning human understanding*, he focused on what he identified as inherent in the changes that things constantly undergo. In this regard, he noted that a number of "qualities and substances" come into being "through the operations of other things", which led him to derive his conceptualisation of cause and effect (Locke 2017 [1690], 111):

> We use the general name 'cause' for whatever produces any simple or complex idea, and 'effect' is our name for what is produced [...]. Whatever we consider as conducing to, or operating to bring into existence, any particular simple idea or substance or mode that didn't before exist, we take to be a cause and we label it accordingly. So a cause is what makes some other thing–either simple idea, substance or mode–come into existence; and an effect is what is brought into existence by some other thing.

More than a century later, Archbishop Whately (1853 [1828]) included causality in his division of arguments based on the purposes for which they are advanced in context. In discussing arguments from cause to effect, therefore, he referred to the relation existing between premises, which serve as causes, and conclusions, which describe effects. In more detail, "as far, then, as any cause, popularly speaking, has a tendency to produce a certain effect," Whately (1853 [1828], 44) pointed out, "so far its existence is an argument for that of the effect. If the cause be fully *sufficient*, and no *impediments* intervene, the effect in question follows certainly; and the nearer we approach to this the stronger the argument".

In contemporary argumentation theory, causal argumentation is postulated to occur when "the argument is presented as if what is stated in the argumentation is a means to, a way to, an instrument for or some other kind of causative factor for the standpoint or *vice versa*" (Van Eemeren and Grootendorst 1992, 97). As such, causal argumentation may be observed in a wide array of settings, including those where a prediction is made and, as with the reverse variant of the argument, in order to defend the standpoint that something is or must have been the case, by introducing a factual event as the result of what is stated in the standpoint. In keeping with the pragma-dialectical approach, Van Eemeren et al. (2002, 101) schematize causal argumentation as follows:

> Y is true of X
> because Z is true of X
> and Z leads to Y

The articulation of causality in the form of pragmatic argumentation has been thoroughly examined by Feteris (2016) in judicial settings. In legal justification, the general argument scheme of pragmatic argumentation may be observed to be embedded in an argumentative pattern of complex argumentation. The complexity of the argumentation is related to the contribution of pragmatic argumentation to justification in cases where the acceptability of the application of a legal rule in a specific interpretation is defended. In order to investigate the argumentative patterns developing from the extension of pragmatic argumentation in response to critical questions, Feteris (2016) argues that the desirability or undesirability of a specific decision tends to be assessed in the light of the goal of the rule.

Since legal rules can be seen as a means to reach objectives that are desirable from a legal, social, or economic perspective, an interpretation that relates to the goal of the rule may be identified as a relevant form of justification. The most authoritative source to reconstruct the goal of the rule is the historical legislator's original intention when they laid down the rule. The goal of the rule may ultimately rest on the explicit intention of the legislator, as can be assumed from legislative documents, which Feteris (2016, 67) refers to as "subjective teleological interpretation of the meaning of the rule". Alternatively, the court may opt for the objective goal of the rule, which requires going back to the rationale of the rule in the context of the law as a whole.

To maintain that the application of the rule is acceptable in a subjective teleological or objective teleological interpretation, a second level of subordinate argumentation should be identified. In turn, this denotes the argumentation that the desirability or undesirability of the consequences in relation to the purpose or goal of the rule can be asserted. In legal theory, the argumentation referring to the goal or purpose is typically advanced as argumentation from coherence with a range of legal approaches, purposes, policies, principles and values. The centrality of such components to judicial reasoning may vary according to the legal system under analysis. In the following section, an overview is provided of the practices of judicial interpretation commonly employed in the Republic of Ireland.

2.5.3 Interpreting the law in the Republic of Ireland

As in other countries, the justification of judicial decisions in Ireland is closely correlated with the adoption of canons of interpretation invoked by courts in judgments. Supplemented though they are by a variety of devices used in the course of interpretation (e.g. presumption of constitutionality, compatibility with EU as well as international law and others), the principal approaches to judicial interpretation in the Irish legal order are essentially twofold, i.e. the literal and the schematic or teleological approach (Byrne et al. 2014).

First of all, the literal approach is accounted for as a modern concept of the more ancient literal rule "which emerged in the 19th century as the preferred method of interpretation" (Byrne et al. 2014, 642). As the primary principle through which legal norms are construed, the literal approach requires judges to assign the ordinary and natural meaning to words, while at once deriving meaning from the context in which words themselves appear. Notwithstanding its apparent simplicity, therefore, the literal approach necessitates that a careful balance be kept between relevant factors. This becomes obvious in two sets of circumstances related to technical meanings to be attached to words. To begin with, context constrains literal meaning in the case of legal terms of art that do not as such bear any ordinary meaning. In addition, the literal approach needs to be mediated by competing factors when legal norms are directed at a distinct group of people rather than society at large, so that the words are interpreted in the way that would be understood by the segment of society involved.

Secondly, the schematic or teleological approach arises as an alternative option as highlighted by Byrne et al. (2014, 647):

> Where the possibility of an absurdity arises a court may reject the literal interpretation and attribute to the words a secondary, modified meaning which they are capable of bearing. In adopting an alternative the court may examine the provision in its wider statutory context and take into account the perceived defect of the pre-existing law.

When the schematic approach is applied, judges take into account the purpose and scheme of legislation. This may entail examining the long title of an Act of the *Oireachtas*, its subject matter and scope, and the pre-existing norms it was conceived to replace or amend. By actually reading words into the law under interpretation, judges thus identify the purpose of a provision and interpret it in a way that is in line with its goals and avoid absurdity. As Byrne et al. (2014) argue, the key point of the schematic interpretation lies in the fact that to interpret the law literally would fail to give effect to the assumed intention of the legislature. Having said that, the schematic approach is characterised by a somewhat high degree of complexity, at least in so far as "the identification of an absurdity leaves an element of discretion to the courts and, to this extent, they are in a position of exercising choice as to the meaning to be attributed to the provision" (Byrne et al. 2014, 651).

From a discourse perspective, judges' tendency to exert discretionary powers in order to balance interpretive approaches, as we saw with canons of constitutional interpretation in Chapter 1, may have far-reaching implications in terms of the use of preferred argument schemes. In Chapter 6, the analysis shows that Feteris's (2016) theorisation of pragmatic argumentation applies well to Article 26 judgments, too, as Supreme Court

Justices are required to establish whether proposed legislation is compatible with or repugnant to the Constitution. At the beginning of the chapter, more details are provided about the nature of the judgments instantiated by the corpus, while the findings reveal which variants of pragmatic argumentation are most commonly present in the Court's reasoning, and how they respond to the critical question(s) discussed in Feteris's research as well.

2.6 Conclusions

This chapter concludes the first part of the volume. While Chapter 1 focused on the key topic addressed by the research, namely the Constitution, its background and defining characteristics, here the aim was to lay the theoretical foundations of the study of the *Bunreacht* and its role in the Irish public sphere. As the title of the chapter suggests, what the book proposes to adopt is a comprehensive, integrated approach sharing the insights provided by a variety of research fields and/or methodologies.

To begin with, corpus linguistics tools will be used to study the constitutional text, identify patterns of linguistic regularity and their function in context. The analysis will be mainly quantitative, although the Irish Constitution is a somewhat limited data set, which will leave space for qualitative interpretation, too. On the other hand, the investigation of argumentative discourse in both the Irish national press and Supreme Court judgments will be inherently qualitative. Based on corpora though the study is, the argument schemes through which the Constitution is "argued" in different ways by journalists, and incorporated in Justices' interpretation of bills of the *Oireachtas*, are retrieved and reconstructed manually.

While the idea of implementing corpus techniques such as concordancing in relation to a constitution is not entirely novel (cf. Partington 2003 on the study of agency in the American Constitution), the large-scale systematic study of constitutional text remains a task scholarly research has yet to seriously engage with. Moreover, historical news analysis is a well-covered research area, the utilisation of qualitative methods has already been called for in approaching news texts (Conboy 2006; Fürsich 2009; Mazzi 2019), and a general overview of the reaction of the press to the introduction of the *Bunreacht* in Ireland as well as in Britain has been provided by the literature (Keogh and McCarthy 2007, 197-199). However, the reconstruction of argument patterns in news discourse from a historical perspective is still relatively unchartered territory. Finally, the investigation of forms of argument, particularly pragmatic argumentation, in judicial discourse has been a well-established acquisition of argumentation studies for years, as we saw in Subsection 2.5.2. Nonetheless, there seems a need to broaden analytical perspectives by interrogating data sets beyond the individual text.

Taken together, Chapters 3-6 constitute an attempt to engage in the task of filling these gaps. To begin with, Chapter 3 is about the materials on which the analysis is based, and the methodological parameters chosen for the study. First of all, the chapter will go through the process of corpus design, i.e. how many texts and word forms the corpora include, the time span covered by the collected data, whether the corpora are of a synchronic or diachronic type, and any text inclusion or exclusion requirements. Secondly, the chapter will illustrate the various stages through which the analysis was carried out. The focus will therefore be on the combination of corpus and discourse tools, and the practical application of the quantitative and qualitative methods already foreshadowed by this chapter in more detail.

CHAPTER THREE

MATERIALS AND METHODS

3.1 Introduction

Chapter 1 served the purpose of introducing readers to the main features of the Irish Constitution, whose historical background was provided and whose most controversial and at once fascinating aspects were discussed. In Chapter 2, the research undertaken here on *Bunreacht na hÉireann* was set out in the light of the wide range of approaches integrated in the volume, from corpus linguistics to argumentation theory. In this chapter, the foundations are established for the presentation of findings later in the volume. To begin with, corpus design criteria are laid down in Section 3.2. Accordingly, details are provided about the parameters through which texts were collected and the characteristics of each of the collected corpora (Subsections 3.2.1-3.2.3). Secondly (3.3), methodological issues are dealt with, with the aim of making the stages explicit at which the analysis was performed. In that regard, the interplay of quantitative analysis with qualitative interpretation is discussed in detail (Subsections 3.3.1-3.3.3) for each and every research strand of Chapters 4-6. In this respect, the case is made for an overall two-pronged approach, where quantitative corpus analysis is followed by and combined with qualitative discourse findings. The chapter is thus first and foremost concerned with issues of procedure, whereas the ones that follow will be entirely devoted to evidence.

3.2 Materials: Criteria for corpus design

3.2.1 *Bunreacht na hÉireann* as a corpus

In Chapter 4, the Constitution of Ireland itself is the corpus. Ever since the *Bunreacht* was introduced, the text has been amended multiple times. It is important to note, therefore, that the most recent version was used for the purpose of our study. This is available from the official website of the Irish Government at https://www.gov.ie/en/publication/d5bd8c-constitution-of-ireland/ (last accessed: 12 March 2020), where the full text can be downloaded either as a pdf or in HTML format. Since the Constitution was also examined through computer-based methods (cf. Subsection 3.3.1), the text was downloaded and converted into a txt file compatible with the linguistic software package implemented later on.

As far as the present investigation is concerned, the various amendments *per se* were not taken into account. As a result, the short paragraphs describing each amendment, such as "Ninth Amendment of the Constitution Act, 1984 *[Extended the right to vote at Dáil elections to certain non-Irish nationals.]*", were excluded as they were not immediately relevant to the analysis. Rather, since the substance of the changes they effected has been incorporated into the main text of the Constitution, not least in terms of its wording, only the running text of the *Bunreacht* was considered. Overall, the English version of the Constitution, on which the research focuses, consists of 50 Articles and 16,592 word forms.

3.2.2 The *Bunreacht_News Corpus*

In Chapter 5, the focus shifts to the presence of the Constitution in the Irish public sphere. In particular, in order to assess how the enactment of the *Bunreacht* was discussed and received at a popular level, a corpus of news texts from Ireland's national press was compiled. As is explained in Section 5.1, the two newspapers considered for a comparative analysis were the *Irish Independent* and the *Irish Press*: the former had gradually taken over the *Freeman's Journal*'s leadership as a nationalist newspaper in the first two decades of the twentieth century, while the *Press* was launched in 1931 as a publication to boost the profile of de Valera and his party, *Fianna Fáil*, ahead of a major turning point for post-Independence Ireland, namely the 1932 general election.

In order to design the corpus, the two newspapers were accessed through the official website of the Irish Newspaper Archives,[1] the world's largest and oldest online database of Irish newspapers. The archives allow one to browse through the pages of a large number of Irish newspapers from 1738 until the current day. It is an extremely authoritative source, and researchers looking for any issue of the national or local newspapers it includes through the National Library of Ireland's catalogue are re-directed to the Archives, where access is granted upon subscription. Through the Archives' website, it is possible to launch a search for articles by inserting a keyword or name, the title of a publication, and the dates

---

[1] Irish News Archives. N.d. Accessed December 12, 2019. https://www.irishnewsarchive.com.

within which one wishes the search to be conducted. In our case, the *Independent* and the *Press* were searched between 1 July 1937, i.e. the day of the plebiscite (cf. Section 1.2), and 31 December of the same year, namely a few days in the wake of its formal enactment. The texts were obtained by using *Constitution* and its Irish equivalent *Bunreacht* as search terms.

By applying these parameters, the Archives displayed the headlines or the first few lines of the retrieved news texts, ordered by means of a relevance coefficient. Although the coefficient worked fairly well, each text was carefully scrutinised in order to assess whether it should be included in the corpus. A total of 50 texts were thus selected for each newspaper as those that more thoroughly discussed the contents and properly assessed the historical and cultural significance of the new Constitution. Taken together, the 100 texts eventually included formed the so-called *Bunreacht_News* corpus.

3.2.3 The *SCI_26 Corpus*

Chapter 6 addresses the issue of the relationship between *Bunreacht na hÉireann* and the Irish public sphere at a specialised level. As such, it was based on a corpus of Supreme Court of Ireland judgments on Article 26 references. As we briefly anticipated in Section 2.5 and will see in more detail in 6.1, these are the judgments the Court delivers on the constitutionality of proposed legislation, upon the President's request. In order to collect the so-called *SCI_26* corpus, the Court's official website was accessed at http://www.supremecourt.ie as of 31 January 2020, when corpus design was completed. On the homepage, the link *Judgments* redirects one to a dedicated webpage from which the Court's jurisprudence can be accessed.

In the main, analysts may avail of the advanced-search function allowing one to insert any word or word string in the quest for judgments. In our case, however, the link *Article 26 judgments* was the clue to access a more specific page on which the whole of the Supreme Court's judgments in this area were listed. The 15 full texts displayed on this page cover a time span between 1940 and 2005, when President Mary McAleese last referred a bill to the Supreme Court under Article 26. These texts were collected to generate a corpus that altogether amounts to 201,134 words.

3.3 Methodology

The methods of this study were devised in an attempt to address the research questions outlined in Section 1.1. The articulation of the methodological approach follows the prior section as a model. The analytical techniques are therefore presented below in three distinct subsections. Each one of these corresponds to the related subsection in 3.2 so that, for instance, 3.3.1 presents the methods through which the Constitution was analysed as a corpus; 3.3.2 outlines the criteria through which the *Bunreacht_News* corpus of 3.2.2 was investigated; and in 3.3.3, the procedure for the analysis of the *SCI_26* corpus (cf. 3.2.3) is described.

3.3.1 A corpus study of *Bunreacht na hÉireann*

In order to select the lexical items to be analysed through corpus methods, data may be processed in more than one way (cf. Section 2.2). For the purpose of choosing a representative data set from the Constitution, we combined various tools that intersected at the outset of the investigation, as it were. First and foremost, we generated a wordlist and looked at the first 100 items on it, in an attempt to establish any regularity between one word form and the next. An in-depth overview of the list revealed that, among the content words included, a non-negligible amount belonged to a circumscribed set of lexical fields. For instance, there were a few words that shared a normative sematic trait, so to speak–e.g., *Article*, *Bill* and *Act*.

With the aim of triangulating this first-hand evidence with other data-mining methods, an n-gram list was generated for both 4-grams and 5-grams, while a keyword list was obtained by comparing the Constitution's wordlist with the 1m-word Irish section of a General-English corpus, namely *ICE-Ireland*.[2] When it was noted that most of the same word forms as in the wordlist also appeared in the 4/5-gram list and the keyword list, those words associated with the most-widely represented lexical fields were eventually taken as a data set to proceed with a more fine-grained analysis.

The selected word forms were then examined in context. In order to do so, they were concordanced and re-sorted to various degrees on the left and the right of the node. As we saw in the previous chapter, such systematic way of looking at the whole of the occurrences of each word

---

[2] *ICE_Ireland* is available under licence from: http://ice-corpora.net/ice/index.html (Last accessed: 25 March 2020).

enables one to identify reiterated patterns of co-selection corresponding to well-defined discourse functions. In particular, regularity in the data was revealed by looking at each term's collocational trends, while at the same time paying attention to colligation and semantic preference.

The analysis was inherently corpus-driven and quantitative. It was corpus-driven because no pre-determined theoretical framing was applied to the data set, nor were specific lexical items identified at the outset and then searched for on the frequency lists. Rather, word forms were selected on the basis of their recurrence across the lists and regularity was described and accounted for *ex post*. Furthermore, the analysis was quantitative in that it only focused on recognisable discourse functions across the word forms under investigation.

Once four main discourse functions were emphasised through concordance analysis, quantitative trends were also subject to qualitative interpretation. More generally, the quantitative dimension was explored through the computer-based functions of *AntConc 3.2.1* (Anthony 2006), which include both the frequency-list options mentioned earlier on and a concordancer. On the other hand, the qualitative interpretation of findings benefited not only from the insights provided by expert voices close to the studies cited in Chapter 1, but also from an interesting comparative study of the Irish-language version of the *Bunreacht*. Accordingly, for instance, the discourse function lying in the coverage of the law-making powers incumbent on leading figures such as the President and the *Taoiseach* was also evaluated in the light of the extant literature on Ireland's constitutional architecture. Moreover, the cursory look at the Irish version of the Constitution allowed us to focus on specific linguistic choices of no secondary importance, such as that of modality in association with the function of legislative empowerment illustrated in Section 4.3.

3.3.2 A qualitative study of argumentative discourse (I): The *Bunreacht_News Corpus*

While the corpus-driven quantitative side of the research prevails in Chapter 4, the study of both the *Bunreacht_News* and the *SCI_26* corpora was mainly qualitative and corpus-based. In Chapter 5, the investigation focused on the lexical and argumentative strategies through which the two newspapers included in the corpus represent and construct the new Constitution for the respective readership. Unlike in Chapter 4, where computer-assisted methods of language analysis were implemented, the texts in *Bunreacht_News* were examined only manually.

In particular, the stages through which the news texts were approached were as follows. First of all, the whole of the 100 texts in the corpus were read, in order to detect the most widely spread argument schemes (cf. Section 2.3) advanced by *Irish Independent* and *Irish Press* journalists in relation to the Constitution. To begin with, this amounted to reconstructing and schematising each argument, and then looking for more general patterns of multiple or coordinative argumentation that embedded the schemes and formed the overall structure of each newspaper's discourse.

On the one hand, multiple argumentation is observed to be advanced when arguers make more than one attempt to defend their own standpoint. This accounts for an option in implicit discussions too, where the antagonist is not necessarily present and "the arguer can only anticipate an opponent's criticisms" (Snoeck Henkemans 2003, 408). More precisely, multiple argumentation is seen as complex argumentation, whereby "the only connection between the first argument and the new argument is that each of them is advanced as a defence for the same standpoint" (Snoeck Henkemans 2003, 411). Moreover, the arguments advanced do not need each other to adequately support the standpoint: rather, "the only reason for undertaking a new attempt at defending the standpoint is that the previous argument has failed or that the arguer expects that it might fail" (Snoeck Henkemans 2003, 411).

On the other hand, coordinative argumentation is pinpointed where two or more arguments "need each other to provide adequate support for the standpoint" (Snoeck Henkemans 2003, 411), in the hope that the combination of arguments may eventually satisfy the antagonist(s).

In second place, the use of the argument schemes was elucidated at three more levels: the first was that of other rhetorical strategies and at once of repeated lexical choice to maximise the impact of the selected schemes. For instance, evidence was provided of the *Press*' tendency to use language that sensationalises the people's reaction to the introduction of the Constitution, or to cite the endorsement for the *Bunreacht* of prominent figures from the Catholic Hierarchy. The second level at which the analysis shed light on the schemes was by focusing on dominant themes on which the news texts often focused to debate the new charter, e.g. the role of women in Irish society as envisaged in the document. Finally, due care was taken to reconstruct the use of schemes in the news texts where the two newspapers (or people writing from their columns, as in the case of letters to the editor) engaged in critical discussion with each other by addressing the respective arguments and attempting to reverse them.

This kind of multi-layered, detailed investigation was intended to fully unlock the potential of argumentation analysis in bringing the stance and commitments of the *Independent* as well as the *Press* to the fore, as they occupied the national public sphere and debated the text that was to shape the country's public life and social profile from then on.

3.3.3 A qualitative study of argumentative discourse (II): The *SCI_26 Corpus*

In the case study on the impact of the Republic's fundamental law on the judiciary undertaken in Chapter 6, the analysis was, once again, inherently qualitative and corpus-based. From a practical point of view, it was conducted in two main stages. To begin with, the corpus texts were all manually scrutinised with a twofold aim. First of all, text structure was reconstructed, in order to find out how the judgments are organised as well as to identify where the Chief Justice's argumentation can be observed at work. As is often the case with judicial texts, not surprisingly, all texts appeared to conform to the same standard: after a few preliminary steps where, among others, a list of key terms related to the subject areas covered by the bill is provided and the Supreme Court's composition is outlined, the Chief Justice pronounces judgment and puts forward the Court's argumentation. It is on this rather extensive part of the judgments that a second aim was furthered. As for the previous chapter, a quest for the most widely spread argument scheme(s) was pursued, and an overall prevalence of pragmatic argumentation (cf. Subsection 2.5.2) was noted.

The second stage of the investigation lay in subdividing the corpus into two sections: the first was to include judgments in which the Supreme Court pronounced in favour of the constitutionality of proposed legislation, while the second included those judgments where bills were declared repugnant to *Bunreacht na hÉireann*. In each section, the presence of one or more variants of pragmatic argumentation (Van Poppel 2012) was detected, in the attempt to reveal whether any systematic correlation existed between the deployment of specific variants of the argumentation and the decision to uphold or reject the constitutionality of bills. This was pointed out to be the case, and for each variant, Feteris's (2016) study was taken as a reference for the purpose of illustrating how the use of pragmatic argumentation is interwoven with a second level of subordinate argumentation. As will be seen in more detail in Chapter 6, this denotes the argumentation that the desirability or undesirability of the consequences of the proposed interpretation of legislation against the backdrop of the Constitution correlates with a key purpose or goal pursued by the *Bunreacht*'s drafters in response to critical questions.

In order to present the findings from the two stages clearly, a few selected judgments were taken into account, for each of which the factual background to the case was explained in detail. In a bid to make the presentation of the results more captivating, moreover, two cases were discussed more thoroughly by virtue of their newsworthiness and relevance to the Irish politics and society of the time. These were the judgments on the Regulation of Information (Services outside the State for Termination of Pregnancies) Bill 1995, and the Emergency Powers Bill 1976.

3.4 Conclusions

This chapter plays an important role in preparing readers to the findings documented over the next three chapters. While the first part of the chapter (Section 3.2) laid down corpus design criteria, the second part (Section 3.3) presented and justified methodological choices. These were designed to approach the complex issues of the language of the Irish Constitution and its implications for Irish public discourse at both a popular level instantiated by the press, and a specialised level represented by judicial discourse. Taken together, the research directions provided across Section 3.3 were intended to productively combine quantitative findings with qualitative insights, and corpus perspectives with textual inputs on argumentative discourse. As such, they are argued here to establish a workable, integrated and highly flexible methodological framework for the study of the relationship between Ireland's founding charter and the country's public sphere.

A case for a quantitative corpus-assisted study of the *Bunreacht* can be made due to the insights provided by such a systematic analysis. As is shown by the data we share in Chapter 4, this allowed for a fairly comprehensive overview of the Constitution, where the collocational trends of the selected lexical items served as a key to important discourse functions. Interestingly, the findings suggest that by following language clues, as it were, much of what the Constitution is about and the way it conveys meaning can be successfully uncovered.

As regards the merits of qualitative analysis across Chapters 5 and 6, these did not simply amount to a general opportunity to undertake a more detailed investigation of argument schemes and patterns by virtue of the restricted data set we chose for both *Bunreacht_News* and *SCI_26*. More specifically, first of all, the rich harvest of qualitative analysis in association with news texts has been reaped in more than a contribution over the past few years. Accordingly, Fürsich (2009, 240) argues that the method involves serious engagement with the chosen texts through genre and rhetorical approaches, and it enables one to successfully "focus on the underlying ideological and cultural assumptions of the text". In her view, the meticulous reading and contextualised interpretation of the news text are ultimately suited "to textually derive a particular media content's unique […] conditions of production and how […] text positions audiences in specific […] ways" (Fürsich 2009, 248).

Secondly, research on judicial argumentation has mostly been carried out from a qualitative perspective as well. This refers as much to works such as Feteris's (2002 and 2016) on pragmatic argumentation as to the investigation of other argument schemes. For instance, Kloosterhuis's (2005) study of analogy argumentation is a case in point. While in many cases analogy argumentation is reconstructed as a simple form of argumentation consisting of two premises and a conclusion, he sharpens the focus on the question of how to analyse complex analogy argumentation. He therefore undertakes a sample study limited to Dutch case law, in order to discuss criteria to reconstruct complex analogy argumentation, which he evaluates against the backdrop of critical questions and with a view to arguments advanced against a specific analogy argumentation, too.

On the whole, corpus and text were used in this volume as benchmarks for an integrated approach to the discourse of *Bunreacht na hÉireann* and argumentative discourse in the Irish public space between Independence and the present time. In this respect, lexical choices and patterns of argumentative discourse were the cornerstones of the investigation. The findings from the three stages in which the analysis was performed are presented over Chapters 4-6 in the next part of the volume.

CHAPTER FOUR

A CORPUS ANALYSIS OF *BUNREACHT NA HÉIREANN*

4.1 Introduction

This chapter opens the second part of the book. It is devoted to the first strand of findings about the Constitution of Ireland. In this regard, the text of *Bunreacht na hÉireann* is treated as a corpus in its own right, and as such is interrogated in an attempt to establish what regular patters of language use emerge from it as a small database. As we saw in the previous chapter, the investigation was undertaken on a mainly semantic basis. The most frequent word forms were therefore extracted by identifying the dominant lexical fields across the first 100 tokens of the corpus frequency list. The lexical items were then examined in context, in order to highlight two interrelated aspects: the first is the main co-textual company each word keeps, as it were, while the second is the range of textual functions fulfilled by the phraseological units retrieved by looking at collocation itself.

In Section 4.2, a preliminary overview of corpus findings is presented. Accordingly, a list of the most frequent lexical fields along with the related word forms and clusters is provided. In Section 4.3, subsequently, the main functions performed by the selected word forms in context are described in detail. As we shall see, these range from legislative empowerment to a definition of the duties and prerogatives of the key institutional stakeholders acting as the main figures in the polity envisaged by Ireland's constitutional charter.

4.2 *Bunreacht na hÉireann* as a corpus: A preliminary overview

By generating a wordlist for *Bunreacht na hÉireann,* one notes that the first 100 words on the list tend to belong to a well-defined set of lexical fields. These can be broadly accounted for as "norms", "people from the institutions", "the institutions" and "the Irish people". Given the specificity of the Constitution compared to General-English texts, it is not surprising to note that many of the same words appear in the top 100 key items one retrieves by comparing the *Bunreacht* with the written section of the International Corpus of English–Ireland (*ICE–Ireland*). Moreover, the same word forms also occur within the most frequent clusters in the 4/5-gram wordlist produced through *AntConc*. These aspects prompt one to choose the word forms involved as an object of more in-depth analysis and are well illustrated by the sample forms reported in Table 4.1 for each lexical field in the corpus wordlist as well as some of the most common clusters and keywords of the constitutional document:

Table 4.1. Main lexical fields, clusters and keywords in *Bunreacht na hÉireann* and related raw frequency

<table>
<tr><th>Lexical fields
in Bunreacht na hÉireann</th><th>4/5-grams</th></tr>
<tr><td rowspan="3">"Norms": law (148 entries), Article (132), Bill (94), Act (50), Amendment (41), provision (34);

"People from the institutions": President (136 entries), Taoiseach (45), member (43), Chairman (28);

"The institutions": Dáil (93 entries), Court (89), Oireachtas (71), Government (55), Council [of State] (34);

"The Irish people": person (49 entries), people (32), persons (23).</td><td>Houses of the Oireachtas (28 entries)
the Council of State (26)
a member of the (15)
Members of Dáil Éireann (12)
Seanad Éireann shall be (8)
The High Court shall (6)
Chairman of Seanad Éireann (5)</td></tr>
<tr><th>Keywords
(Bunreacht v. ICE–Ireland)</th></tr>
<tr><td>President, law, Dáil, Article, Oireachtas, Seanad, Court, Houses, Amendment, Supreme, Taoiseach, provisions, Chairman, Government, Council</td></tr>
</table>

The fact that a country's fundamental law may be concerned with the task of laying down the rules behind the operation of key institutional players hardly comes as a surprise. The next section applies the study of collocation to the word forms in the lexical fields displayed on the left of Table 4.1, in order to see what notion of democracy is altogether incorporated in the Irish Constitution.

4.3 The words of *Bunreacht na hÉireann* in context: A corpus-driven study

The presence of the same kind of words across frequency and keyword lists may indeed be taken to testify to the centrality of these to the framework set by drafters for the constitutional infrastructure of a new Ireland 15 years after Independence. Nonetheless, the word forms themselves tell us little, if anything at all, about the actual function performed by these terms in the Constitution at large. This section is intended to fill such gap, and it argues that the selected word forms may be accounted for as fulfilling the following interrelated functions: first of all, legislative empowerment, thus bestowing a wide range of prerogatives to the *Oireachtas* as the political representation of the people's voice; secondly, a definition of the people's role in democratic processes in terms of their involvement as well as sovereign rights; thirdly, the allocation of duties to institutions; finally, the in-depth coverage of law-making powers incumbent on leading figures such as the President and the *Taoiseach*.

The first function, i.e. legislative empowerment, refers to the various parts of the constitution where future decisions are envisaged as part of the *Oireachtas*' law-making prerogatives. As the country's fundamental law, it is only fair to expect *Bunreacht na hÉireann* to introduce a high degree of flexibility, so that in its capacity as the spokesperson of the Irish people, so to speak, the *Oireachtas* is empowered to make the decisions needed, whenever the occasion arises in future. This aspect forms the core of many an article of the Constitution, and is reflected by a range of phraseological options regarding the nouns *law* and *provision*. As regards the former, 21.6% of the occurrences of *law* were isolated as mooting this valuable idea, mostly in the form of an appositive clause introduced by *as*.

To begin with, there are a number of areas where the people, items or circumstances to be included in the scope of constitutional norms may be determined at the *Oireachtas*' discretion as necessity dictates. With the exception of the few entries where the modal *shall* is used instead of *may*, this is expressed through chunks such as *as may be determined by law*, *provision may be made by law for/to*, *as may be prescribed by law* and *as may be provided by law*. In these cases, the use of *may* is associated with what Biber et al. (1999) call "intrinsic modality". This "refers to actions and events that humans (or other agents) directly control: meanings relating to permission, obligation, or volition (or intention)" (Biber et al. 1999, 485).

By looking at the use of the above chunks in context, it can be rightly pointed out that they are aimed at granting the *Oireachtas* as the State's legislative body the power to determine who will have the right to vote (example 1 below), what meetings may be prevented or controlled (2), what official purposes make it advisable to encourage the use of only one of the Republic's two official languages (3), the scope of the Supreme Court's jurisdiction (4), and the exceptions to the rule that all revenues of the State be part of one fund (5):[1]

(1) All citizens, and such other persons in the State as may be determined by law, without distinction of sex who have reached the age of eighteen years who are not disqualified by law and comply with the provisions of the law relating to the election of members of Dáil Éireann, shall have the right to vote at an election for members of Dáil Éireann. (Art. 16.1.2)

(2) Provision may be made by law to prevent or control meetings which are determined in accordance with law to be calculated to cause a breach of the peace or to be a danger or nuisance to the general public and to prevent or control meetings in the vicinity of either House of the Oireachtas. (Art. 40.6.1)

(3) 1 The Irish language as the national language is the first official language. 2 The English language is recognised as a second official language. 3 Provision may, however, be made by law for the exclusive use of either of the said languages for any one or more official purposes, either throughout the State or in any part thereof. (Art. 8).

(4) The Supreme Court shall, with such exceptions and subject to such regulations as may be prescribed by law, have appellate jurisdiction from all decisions of the High Court, and shall also have appellate jurisdiction from such decisions of other courts as may be prescribed by law. (Art. 34.4.3)

(5) All revenues of the State from whatever source arising shall, subject to such exception as may be provided by law, form one fund, and shall be appropriated for the purposes and in the manner and subject to the charges and liabilities determined and imposed by law. (Art. 11)

Why is discretion so important in contexts such as those denoted by the passages in (1)-(5)? Based on a closer look at (2) and (3), for instance, it

[1] For every numbered example, the phraseological item of interest is underlined, while the article of the Irish Constitution the text is taken from is indicated in brackets at the end of each example.

may be suggested that it is hardly possible to establish, once and for all, what represents a *breach of the peace, a danger or nuisance to the general public*, as the people's tolerance limit is likely to change dramatically over the years. Similarly, it seems very difficult to foresee what official purposes would advise the authorities to prefer English to Irish or vice versa, not least because the number of Irish-language speakers of 1937 was radically different from that of 2020 Ireland. Finally, since decisions about the compilation of voting records and how to undertake judicial reform are also susceptible to varying according to needs and circumstances, it is important for the Constitution to make room for the flexibility that is required.

Interestingly, there tends to be no absolute consistency between the English text of the Constitution and its Irish counterpart. Although this work could hardly be seen as a contrastive cross-linguistic study of the Constitution, the fact that the Irish text is established to prevail in case of conflict (Article 25.5.4) makes comparisons of this kind almost inevitable. In his seminal work on the Irish version of *Bunreacht na hÉireann*, Ó Cearúil (1999) notes that the Irish language itself is hardly consistent on the matter. In fact, he suggests that the various ways in which *shall* and *may* are expressed in Irish are a feature that aptly illustrates that the Irish text does not quite qualify as a mere translation of the English version (cf. Section 1.7).

To be more precise, the two versions of the Constitution often differ with a view to modality. On the one hand, English prefers *may* and as a result stresses permission and empowerment, as we saw in the excerpts discussed earlier on. On the other hand, Irish chooses between two options: either it adds a sense of urgency to the text by choosing a future tense somewhere half-way between "volition/prediction" and "obligation/necessity" (Biber et al. 1999, 485), as is the case with the equivalent of *as may be determined by law* and *as may be prescribed by law*, or it expresses tentativeness and permission, as in the Irish version of *provision may be made by law* closer to the English text.

Thus, the relevant passages in (1) and (4) in Irish respectively read as follows: *Gach uile shaoránach, agus cibé daoine eile sa Stát* ***a cinnfear le dlí…*** [Every citizen, and any other persons in the State **that will be determined by law…**]; *Taobh amuigh de cibé eisceachtaí agus faoi chuimsiú cibé rialacha* ***a ordófar le dlí****, beidh dlínse achomhairc ag an gCúirt Uachtarach ar bhreitheanna uile na hArd-Chúirte agus, fairis sin, ar na breitheanna sin ó chúirteanna eile* ***a ordófar le dlí*** [Apart from any exceptions and under any regulations **that will be prescribed by law**, the Supreme Court will have rights of appeal on any judgment of the High

Court and, along with that, on those judgments from other courts **that will be prescribed by law**].

By reading through the almost word-for-word translation provided above, one would be tempted to believe that the realisation of empowerment through permission we have seen for English is altogether absent from Irish. This, however, does not hold true for all contexts of use. In fact, this is the Irish-language equivalent of *provision may be made by law* in (2) and (3) above, respectively: ***Féadfar socrú a dhéanamh de réir dlí*** *chun cosc a chur nó rialú a dhéanamh ar thionóil…*[**Provision may be made by law** to prohibit or control meetings…]; *Ach* ***féadfar socrú a dhéanamh le dlí*** *d'fhonn ceachtar den dá theanga sin a bheith ina haonteanga le haghaidh…*[But **provision may be made by law** in order for either of the two languages to be the only language for the purpose of…]. A wholly literal translation was not possible here, since Irish applies the passive particle *-far* to the modal–*féad* [be able to]–rather than to *make* (*déan*). However, Ó Cearúil confirms that *to make provision* is generally expressed as *socrú a dhéanamh* across *Bunreacht na hÉireann*.

Overall, Ó Cearúil (1999, 13) argues that "divergences between the two texts" should be interpreted "as being due more to a deliberate effort on the part of the drafters of the Irish text to make that text read independently of the English text and to provide a text in natural Irish", complying with generalised usage patterns of the language "rather than sacrificing the language to achieve exact correspondence with the English text". To this remark we might add that collocational surroundings appear to influence the choice of the modal involved. This is the case to the extent that within the same norm, English may distinguish *as may be determined by law* from *as shall be determined by law*, whereas Irish renders them both with a passive form introduced by *will*. In other words, a readily available equivalent of *may be + PP* exists yet is tied to the cluster *provision may be made by law* and is somehow dispreferred as the Irish variant of *as may be determined/prescribed by law*, as demonstrated by example (6) below:

(6) Every citizen who has the right to vote at an election for members of Dáil Éireann and such other persons as may be determined by law shall have the right to vote at an election for members of such of the local authorities referred to in section 2 of this article as shall be determined by law. (Art. 28A.4)

Gach saoránach ag a bhfuil ceart vótála i dtoghchán comhaltaí do Dháil Éireann agus cibé daoine eile ***a chinnfear le dlí****, beidh ceart vótála acu i dtoghchán comhaltaí cibé údaráis áitiúla dá dtagraítear in alt 2 den airteagal seo* ***a chinnfear le dlí****.* [Every citizen who has a voting right in an election for members to Dáil Éireann and any other persons **that will be determined by law**, will have a voting right in an election for members of whatever local authority to which reference is made in section 2 of this article **that will be determined by law**].

A much less frequent option is the passive form of the present tense, whose distribution is only restricted to the very few (5 altogether) occurrences of *as may be provided by law*, from the items underlined in examples (1)-(5). The Irish version of the relevant bit from (5) earlier on is therefore as follows: *Ní foláir cíos uile an stáit cibé bunadh atá leis, ach amháin an chuid sin de* ***ar a ndéantar eisceacht le dlí****, a chur in aon chiste amháin*...[Every revenue of the State from whatever origin it is, with the exception of that part **on which exception is made by law**, shall be put into one fund].

From a merely quantitative point of view, finally, the 6-gram *provision may be made by law* is a prime example of intercollocation of collocates. It can be seen both as resulting from the collocation of *law*, which is the way it was originally accounted for, and as a favourite collocational choice for *provision*. In this regard, the cluster gains increased prominence, because it concerns 23.5% of the whole of the occurrences of *provision* in *Bunreacht na hÉireann*.

The second function that could be associated with the use of the selected word forms in context is the definition of the people's role in democratic processes in terms of their involvement as well as sovereign rights. Not surprisingly, this is attached to the use of *person/s* and *people*. As the counterpart of the flexibility granted to the *Oireachtas* through the phraseological units discussed so far, for a start, the occurrence of both the singular and the plural form of *person* is tangible proof of the necessity to attain precision and all-inclusiveness, or avoid ambiguity, in constitutional norms. In 24.6% of their joint entries, therefore, *person/s* collocates with *no*, *every*, *all* or *any*, and thereby secures the fulfilment of these objectives, as can be appreciated from examples (7) and (8):

(7) It is the entitlement and birthright of <u>every person</u> born in the island of Ireland, which includes its islands and seas, to be part of the Irish Nation. That is also the entitlement of <u>all persons</u> otherwise qualified in accordance with law to be citizens of Ireland. Furthermore, the Irish nation cherishes its special affinity with people of Irish ancestry living abroad who share its cultural identity and heritage. (Art. 2)

(8) Treason shall consist only in levying war against the State, or assisting any State or person or inciting or conspiring with <u>any</u>

> person to levy war against the State, or attempting by force of arms or other violent means to overthrow the organs of government established by this Constitution, or taking part or being concerned in or inciting or conspiring with any person to make or to take part or be concerned in any such attempt. (Art. 39)

In (7), the goal of maximum all-inclusiveness is reached in relation to the notion of Irish citizenship. This is an ever relevant part of the Constitution in the light of Ireland's history of emigration and diaspora, and the resulting attempt to create favourable conditions for a broader concept of Irish nationality. This is ensured by formulations such as *every person* and *all persons* in association with the noun *entitlement*. Accordingly, all ambiguity is resolved as to the birthright of everyone born on Irish soil including islands and seas to Irish citizenship. Furthermore, the entitlement of everyone qualifying as an Irish national based on any other requirement laid down by the law is equally emphasised.

The significance and overall impact of Article 39 as in (8) should be equally appreciated. Establishing what *treason* was must have been particularly important in the context of an independent Ireland, the new State designed by the Constitution asserting itself as a result of the painstaking process of nation building that unfolded in the wake of the ever poignant images of civil war and militant republicanism only about fifteen years before.

In (8), the exhaustive definition of *treason* proposed by the norm is stretched to its limits by the use of *any* alongside a lengthy multinomial (Bhatia 1993). Multinomials are sequences of three or more items from the same part of speech joined by punctuation or the conjunctions *and* or *or*. In (8), the multinomial is of a quintessentially verbal nature–i.e., *in levying war [...] or assisting or inciting or conspiring with [...] or attempting [...], or taking part or being concerned in or inciting or conspiring with [...] to make or to take part or be concerned in...*–to add to the inclusivity of the norm. Taken together, the passages in (7) and (8) may be read in the light of the attempt to establish as clearly as possible eligibility criteria for inclusion in the Irish democratic polity (through citizenship), or complete exclusion from it (by way of treason).

As for the space made by the Constitution for the sovereignty of the Irish people, this is arguably an overriding theme in *Bunreacht na hÉireann*. As we saw in Chapter 1 (Section 1.3), the principle of sovereignty is incorporated in the Constitution as early as Article 1, where the Irish nation is singled out as affirming "its inalienable, indefeasible and sovereign right" to choose its own form of government, determine its relations with other nations as well as "develop its life, political, economic and cultural, in accordance with its own genius and traditions". After a protracted national struggle to affirm its political and cultural independence from Britain, it was of paramount importance to stress Ireland's claim to sovereignty in its new fundamental law, thereby celebrating a proud heritage from such texts as the Irish version of the 1916 Proclamation as well as Patrick Pearse's *The Sovereign People* also from 1916 (Ó Cearúil 1999, 59).

Ó Cearúil's analysis of the Irish text of *Bunreacht na hÉireann* deals with the etymology and cultural resonance of the Irish equivalents of the adjectives *inalienable*, *indefeasible* and *sovereign*, namely *doshannta*, *dochloíte* and *ceannasach*. On the other hand, we may gain insights into the centrality of sovereignty to the charter by looking at the main collocational pattern of *people*. In 37.5% of its tokens, *people* collocates with items sharing a semantic preference of "willingness" resting in the Irish people's hands, i.e. *decision*, *consent*, *will* and *approved by*, as can be seen from (9) below:

(9) A majority of the members of Seanad Éireann and not less than one-third of the members of Dáil Éireann may by a joint petition addressed to the President by them under this Article request the President to decline to sign and promulgate as a law any Bill to which this article applies on the ground that the Bill contains a proposal of such national importance that <u>the will of the people</u> thereon ought to be ascertained. (Art. 27.1)

Passages such as (9) deserve to be considered as identifying defining traits of *Bunreacht na hÉireann*. Not only is the Republic of Ireland "one of the few countries where every constitutional amendment requires the consent of the people" (Gallagher 2005, 80), as was required by the country's accession to the European Economic Community, the legalisation of divorce, the fulfilment of the 1998 Good Friday Agreement, the removal of the recognition of the Roman Catholic Church's special position and, most recently, the Eighth Amendment imposing a ban on women's decision to terminate pregnancies. In (9), the Constitution also fosters a strong link between the people's representatives (TDs as well as Senators) and the people themselves, whose *will* can be ascertained should a Bill be deemed to contain a proposal of cardinal national importance.

The third function that appeared to be served by the word forms in Table 4.1 is the allocation of duties to State institutions. This is secured by a number of co-occurrence patterns of *law*, but also of *bill*, *Council [of State]*, *Dáil [Éireann]*, *Oireachtas* and *Court*. In 10.2% of its entries, to begin with, *law* collocates with the complex prepositional phrase *in accordance with*. Further to its left, *law* colligates with verbs sharing a semantic preference of "procedure", e.g. *hold*, *determine* and *regulate*. It is noteworthy that these verbs are invariably used in the passive form introduced by *shall* (see example 10 below). Of note, the co-occurrence with *shall* is also attested for the cluster *in the manner provided by law* (example 11), which in turn concerns 3.4% of the corpus tokens of *law* itself:

(10) The future acquisition and loss of Irish nationality and citizenship shall be determined in accordance with law. (Art. 9.1.3)

(11) Casual vacancies in the number of the elected members of Seanad Éireann shall be filled in the manner provided by law. (Art. 18.10.3)

The role of *shall* in legal texts has been the object of much scholarly discussion and research. On the one hand, for instance, Palmer (1988, 141-142) defines *shall* as a tool that "does not permit or oblige someone else, usually the addressee, to act, but guarantees that the speaker will act": as such, it is "deontic in the essential characteristic that it influences or directs behaviour". Indeed, the meaning of *shall* has all too often been taken for granted as being both deontic and agent-oriented. Laws, regulations and commands have therefore been interpreted as inherently directive, namely as rules that unquestionably influence people's future course of action.

On the other hand, Garzone (2001) suggests that a performative meaning coexists with the deontic nature of *shall*. To a certain degree, this also characterises the forms of *shall* in (10) and (11) above, where a state of things is described that will construct reality upon the passing of relevant legislation. As a result, the enactment of law on citizenship and *Seanad Éireann* will have a discernible impact on reality in that it will introduce the constituent elements for the acquisition or loss of Irish nationality, and the filling of vacant seats in the Republic's upper Chamber, respectively. Consistent with Garzone's (2001, 157) argument, therefore, "the verb forms in such sentences do not predicate any obligation nor any duty to be imposed on anyone; they are definitely not agent-oriented. Rather, they bring about a new state of things or a modification" in a previous state of affairs.

From a conceptual point of view, the prescriptive and performative uses of *shall* share two features: one is that both require a source of authority for the meaning to be appropriately conveyed, while the other is that the predicate is future-oriented. There is, however, a difference in terms of degree. The deontic *shall* imposes an obligation on an agent entrusted with the completion of the designated action. Even though, therefore, it entails that it is up to the source of authority to ensure the fulfilment of the obligation, "there always remains some scope, albeit minimum, for failure to perform, while a constitutive utterance, on the contrary, implies the contextual fulfilment of the action predicated" (Garzone 2001, 167). Crucially, the presence or absence of an agent tells deontic uses apart from performative ones. On the one hand, the deontic use of the modal presupposes agent-orientedness. On the other, *shall* is only performative in the absence of an agent, especially an animate one as in (10) and (11), where the subjects are *future acquisition and loss* and *casual vacancies*, respectively.

As far as *bill* and *Council [of State]* are concerned, the two nouns were observed to be often embedded in passages where in fact the Irish President's duties are set out. That this was done with care in the Irish Constitution should not come as a surprise. The President as we know it nowadays was a figure introduced by *Bunreacht na hÉireann*. As the State's highest representative, the President enjoys both discretionary and non-discretionary powers (Elgie and Fitzgerald 2015). The latter include the duty to appoint the *Taoiseach* as well as the sound practice of being briefed by *Taoisigh* themselves on domestic and international policy. Conversely, discretionary powers to be exercised with somewhat greater freedom include referring a bill to the Supreme Court for a decision on its constitutionality and the right to refuse to dissolve the *Dáil* "on the advice of a Taoiseach who has ceased to retain the support of a majority in Dáil Éireann" (Art. 13.2.2).

From a discursive point of view, the President's prerogatives are frequently detailed through a hypothetical structure established by the literature to be common to the vast majority of legal sentences, namely "if X, then Z shall be Y" or, alternatively, "if X, then Z shall do Y". Notwithstanding possible variations on the basic theme, the "if X" component is essential: as Crystal and Davy (1969, 203) pointed out, "every action or requirement, from a legal point of view, is hedged around with, and even depends upon, a set of conditions which must be satisfied before anything can happen".

The above discourse structure applies to 13.8% of the occurrences of *bill*, where *if* is sometimes replaced by *as soon as*, *where*, *in every case*, *when* or *whenever* (example 12). Moreover, "if X, then Z shall do Y" is attested in 32.4% of the entries of *Council [of State]* (13):

(12) *In every case* in which the President decides that a Bill the subject of a petition under this Article contains a proposal of such national importance that the will of the people thereon ought to be ascertained,

he shall inform the Taoiseach and the Chairman of each House of the Oireachtas accordingly in writing under his hand and Seal and shall decline to sign and promulgate such Bill as a law unless and until the proposal shall have been approved either

(i) by the people at a Referendum in accordance with the provisions of section 2 of Article 47 of this Constitution within a period of eighteen months from the date of the President's decision, or

(ii) by a resolution of Dáil Éireann passed within the said period after a dissolution and re-assembly of Dáil Éireann. (Art. 27.5.1)

(13) *If* the President *after consultation with the* Council of State decides not to accede to the request of Seanad Éireann, or if the Committee of Privileges fails to report within the time hereinbefore specified the certificate of the Chairman of Dáil Éireann shall stand confirmed. (Art. 22.2.6)

The excerpt in (12) is a prime example of legal syntax. As a matter of fact, the first paragraph of the fifth section of Article 27 is phrased as a single sentence. As such, it is characterised by high lexical density (139 words altogether) in the attempt to be as all-inclusive as possible in specifying how *a proposal of such national importance* must be approved in order for the President to sign and promulgate the related bill. As is often the case with provisions like this, the demand for precision creates a curious paradox: the more clarity drafters want to add to the norm, the more details they are likely to include; the more details have been included, the more complex the norm itself turns out to be. It would seem, in other words, that clarity or at least all-inclusiveness may come at the expense of simplicity.

Procedural requirements are also the core of (13). More specifically, Article 22 lays down that the *Ceann Comhairle* (Chairman of *Dáil Éireann*) is to certify any bill he believes to be a money bill as a money bill. Should *Seanad Éireann* choose to do so at a sitting with no less than 30 members, it may pass a resolution requesting the President to refer the question whether the bill is or is not a money bill to a Committee of Privileges. The provision in section 2, paragraph 6, of the Article sets out in which case *the certificate of the Chairman of Dáil Éireann shall stand confirmed.*

In spite of the discourse structure they share, incidentally, (12) and (13) are different because the former features an agent-oriented and deontic use of *shall* clarifying what a President must do in the event that s/he decides that the will of the people should be ascertained on a bill arising from a petition. On the other hand, the use of *shall* in (13) is more definitely on the performative side in that it denotes the state of things–i.e., the Chairman's *certificate* standing–that will become actual fact in case the President *decides not to accede to the request of Seanad Éireann*, or the Committee of Privileges fails to report within the appropriate time frame.

In addition to the President, the Constitution predictably allocates duties to the Irish parliament and defines the jurisdiction of Irish courts. To begin with, 23.6% of the occurrences of *Dáil [Éireann]*–alone or as *Chairman of Dáil Éireann* and *Deputy Chairman of Dáil Éireann*–collocate with deontic *shall* in contexts where the institutional machinery behind parliamentary proceedings is described (example 14). Moreover, *Oireachtas* collocates with *Houses* in 64.8% of its entries. This is hardly surprising, but with specific regard to law-making issues, 26.1% of these are devoted to an in-depth coverage of how legislation is passed by the State's legislative branch (15):

(14) Dáil Éireann *shall* meet within thirty days from that polling day. (Art. 16.4.2)

(15) Every proposal for an amendment of this Constitution shall be initiated in Dáil Éireann as a Bill, and shall upon having been passed or deemed to have been passed by both Houses of the Oireachtas, be submitted by Referendum to the decision of the people in accordance with the law for the time being in force relating to the Referendum. (Art. 46.2)

In (14), the rule is laid down that *Dáil Éireann* has to meet within a month from a general election, whereas (15) outlines the procedure for constitutional amendments: first of all, a dedicated bill has to be initiated in *Dáil Éireann*, passed–or deemed to have been passed, as is the case when the *Dáil* adopts an *ad hoc* resolution to override the *Seanad*'s decision to delay it–by both Houses, and eventually submitted to the people's decision through a referendum. The imperative nature of both provisions is crystal clear as in this case, there is absolute consistency between the English and Irish-language versions. In both, every occurrence of *shall* is translated as *ní foláir*: literally, this is "it is necessary" (Ó Dónaill 1977, 564), it generally renders *must* in Irish and "expresses 'shall' in many Articles" of *Bunreacht na hÉireann* (Ó Cearúil 1999, 13).

Moving from parliament to the judicial branch, the Constitution's drafters obviously devoted full attention to the Irish court system. Needless to say, the noun *Court* takes on different flavours, as it were, depending on the specific court being referred to. In their capacity as courts at the top of the country's judicial hierarchy, the Supreme and High Court are those dealt with most extensively. Taken together as the two top collocates, therefore, *Supreme* and *High* account for 61.8% of the whole of the occurrences of *Court*. A closer look at the related concordance lines reveals that 21.2% of the passages about the Supreme Court concern the way it delivers its own judgments. This is well instantiated by the extract in (16):

(16) *The decision of* the majority of the judges of the Supreme Court shall, for the purposes of this Article, be the decision of the Court and shall be pronounced by such one of those judges as the Court shall direct, and no other opinion, whether assenting or dissenting, shall be pronounced nor shall the existence of any such other opinion be disclosed. (Art. 26.2.2)

In (16), it is stated that in the case of decisions to be pronounced under Article 26 about the compatibility of legislation with the Constitution, the Court has to deliver its verdict as if it were a joint decision by all of the sitting judges, so that neither assenting nor dissenting opinions may be disclosed. This is in sharp contrast with the Court's usual practice, whereby as many assenting or dissenting judgments as are the judges on the bench may be delivered and made public. With specific reference to Article 26 judgments, therefore, the Court's judicial style, so to speak, appears close to the Continental tradition, where "dissent among judges [...] no doubt occurs behind closed doors, but behind those doors it is resolved, and the published motivation is then presented as the single–and, as it might appear–incontestable decision" of the whole court (MacCormick 1978, 171; but cf. also Barrington 1987, 120-121).

In addition, 36.4% of those passages about the High Court tend to focus on the Court's composition and jurisdiction, as is reflected by the collocation with items such as the noun *jurisdiction* in combination with the verbs *invest with* or *extend*, and shown by (17) below. The passage is part of Article 34 devoted to the Irish Courts. In particular, again by relying on the performative value of *shall*, it assigns the High Court a very important role in that its jurisdiction stretches into questions of validity of legislation with regard to constitutional norms:

(17) Save as otherwise provided by this Article, the jurisdiction of the High Court shall extend to the question of the validity of any law having regard to the provisions of this Constitution, and no such question shall be raised (whether by pleading, argument or otherwise) in any Court established under this or any other Article of

this Constitution other than the High Court or the Supreme Court. (Art. 34.3.2)

The fourth and final function identified in association with the word forms prevailing in Table 4.1 lies in an in-depth coverage of the law-making powers incumbent on leading figures such as the President and the *Taoiseach*. The President's figure is one we introduced earlier on, but there is more to say in terms of the collocational features of the corresponding noun. Overall, *President* occurs 136 times in *Bunreacht na hÉireann*. To begin with, it is noteworthy that his/her powers are outlined through passive constructions in 25% of its corpus entries, where it primarily collocates with the fixed noun phrase *power or function*, as in (18) below. As can be seen from the passage, the provision in Article 13.11 essentially limits the President's freedom of action in that his/her functions are subject to the Government's advice. This trend is confirmed by the main collocational pattern of *Government* itself. In 9.1% of its 55 occurrences, the noun collocates with *advice*, *approval, authority* and *consent* within prepositional phrases such as *on the advice of* or *with the consent of*, as in (19) below. By looking at (18) and (19), furthermore, it can be noted that the Government's primacy over the President's figure is clearly established. Both examples are phrased negatively in relation to powers that may not be exerted and actions that may not be performed; both contain one of the above prepositional phrases reinforced by *save*. In (19), accordingly, the use of negation in the verb phrase (*shall not*) expresses prohibition, so that the President may not leave the State without the Government's consent:

(18) No *power or function* conferred on the <u>President</u> by law shall be exercisable or performable by him *save* only *on the advice of the Government*. (Art. 13.11)

(19) The President shall not leave the State during his term of office *save with the consent of the Government*. (Art. 12.9)

As for the *Taoiseach*, s/he is the leading figure of Ireland's executive branch. *Taoisigh* have a wide array of constitutional, administrative and political resources at their disposal. They are entitled to appoint Government members, however subject to *Dáil* approval. In addition, they have a right to appoint the Attorney General, that is the Government's chief legal advisor. They enjoy the power to dissolve the *Dáil* and in their capacity as Heads of Government, they are the real agenda-setters of government action. As such, although they are in a somewhat weaker position in case of coalition let alone minority governments, *Taoisigh* basically retain the power to determine the order in which government business is taken on a daily basis.

From a discourse point of view, it is significant that 24.4% of the corpus tokens of *Taoiseach* collocate with items sharing a semantic preference of "extent of powers", as it were. More explicitly, the term was detected to be embedded in clusters such as *on the advice of the Taoiseach*, *if the Taoiseach so advises*, *if so advised by the Taoiseach*, *in the hands of the Taoiseach, the Taoiseach may at any time* and *for reasons which for him seem sufficient*. In these passages, the width of the *Taoiseach*'s discretion is generally measured again in relation to the President's authority, as in (20) below:

> (20) The President shall accept the resignation of a member of the Government, other than the Taoiseach, <u>if so advised by the Taoiseach</u>. 4° The <u>Taoiseach may at any time, for reasons which to him seem sufficient</u>, request a member of the Government to resign; should the member concerned fail to comply with the request, his appointment shall be terminated by the President <u>if the Taoiseach so advises</u>. (Art. 28.9.3-4)

This is indeed an outstanding example, not only because it shows many of the collocational properties of *Taoiseach* at work at the same time, but also because of its contents. Thus, the provision could not be more straightforward in articulating the principle that the *Taoiseach* may require or, should that be necessary, even force a member of his/her government to resign, the President basically only acknowledging that as a *fait accompli*.

4.4 Conclusions

In this chapter, the Constitution of Ireland has been treated as a corpus and analysed through some of the main tools of corpus linguistics. First of all, therefore, the main content words were extracted from *Bunreacht na hÉireann* by combining a set of criteria: not only were prominent word forms chosen on the grounds of their frequency in the corpus wordlist, 4/5-gram list and keyword list. They were also chosen in that they belong to a number of recognisable lexical fields (Section 4.2). In second place, these word forms were concordanced, i.e. analysed in context, in order to identify their main usage patterns and related discourse functions.

As we saw in Section 4.3, the systematic study of their collocational surroundings allowed us to associate their use with four interrelated functions: first of all, legislative empowerment, thus bestowing a wide range of prerogatives to the *Oireachtas* as the political representation of the people's voice; secondly, a definition of the people's role in democratic processes in terms of their involvement as well as sovereign rights; thirdly, the allocation of duties to institutions; finally, the in-depth coverage of law-making powers incumbent on leading figures such as the President and the *Taoiseach*.

The findings presented earlier on are both quantitatively and qualitatively significant. From a quantitative point of view, collocation served to shed light on the frequency of patterns and phraseological units identified through concordance lines. The expectation that what is frequent is also significant has long been a cornerstone of corpus linguistics (Hunston and Francis 1998) and informed the present research, too. In the case of the current investigation, it may be argued that the Constitution is too small to be considered as a corpus in its own right, so that frequencies are overall somewhat limited. While there is no doubt that *Bunreacht na hÉireann* is far from a multi-million-word corpus, it is apparent that its study revealed "recurrences that are not visible when examining individual texts or even many texts but in isolation" (Gozdz-Roszkowski 2018, 158). This applies to both the selected word forms *per se* and their collocates. Suffice it to think of deontic as opposed to performative uses of *shall*, which could hardly be documented in detail on the basis of huge databases.

Furthermore, not only did the findings establish regularities and/or the intercollocation of the items under scrutiny, but they also served as a starting point for the comparison of the Irish-language equivalents of more than one cluster emerging from the analysis. However circumscribed, the parallel study of constructions of the same kind across the two languages made for an insightful reading of corpus data. This is by no means a contrastive English-Irish study, but the comparison was a meaningful one in so far as it pointed out marked discrepancies between the two languages in the choice of modality. Indeed, as Salkie (2018, 140) rightly points out, "viewing two languages in direct contrast can shed light on each of them, and can bring to light modes of expression which are less obvious in monolingual work".

From a qualitative point of view, the interpretation of the patterns in light of the relevant context contributed to highlighting major aspects of the statehood infrastructure erected by the Constitution. On the one hand, themes such as the centrality of sovereignty granted to the Irish people or the institutional profile of the *Oireachtas* along with the prerogatives of President and *Taoiseach* have long been explored by the literature on Irish politics (Coakley and Gallagher 2005), while the Constitution itself was thoroughly discussed by scholars interested in the Irish legal system more generally (cf. Byrne at al. 2014). In this regard, the findings from this chapter will hardly sound new.

On the other hand, the idea behind the chapter was precisely to achieve results similar to those of specialised studies, by utilising a different method. As Stubbs (2001) argues, it is a significant contribution of corpus work to be able to approach text and perform analyses that bring insights in keeping with the perspectives offered by expert readers such as, in our case, political scientists and jurists. At the same time, the chapter provides language clues that substantiate expert knowledge with a closer look at the discourse features of Ireland's fundamental law.

Thus, for instance, it may be said to be predictable that a Constitution empowers parliament to regulate as diverse a range of processes as those related to people's voting rights or the exclusive use of one of the two official languages for official purposes (examples 1 and 2). Similarly, the wide span of the *Taoiseach*'s powers over the President's (example 20) can be recognised as part of common knowledge in the Republic of Ireland. But how are these meanings expressed through the highly-codified formulaic conventions of legal language? The findings reported above help answer this question.

The chapter does not go into the technicalities of constitutional law yet it can be taken as an example of the way computer-assisted discourse studies may lead non-expert readers to approach a lengthy and complex text such as a constitution, by accessing key information starting from word forms and then moving into their co-text and context. Were a study to be conceived of constitutional discourse more generally, it would be interesting to apply the same method to the constitution of another English-speaking country such as the United States of America. Such a comparative framework is likely to show that similar meanings are conveyed through different forms and/or discourse structures, or alternatively that forms and/or discourse structures of the same kind communicate different meanings.

A joint reading of Chapter 1 and this chapter is supposed to satisfy the curiosity of readers interested in the distinctive institutional implications behind and discourse features of *Bunreacht na hÉireann*. The following chapters will now shift our perspective to the public reception and institutional application, as it were, of Ireland's charter.

In Chapter 5, a comparative analysis is conducted of the 1937 issues of two national newspapers (*Irish Independent* and *Irish Press*), in order to document how they reacted to the enactment of the *Bunreacht*, they presented it to the respective readership and they "argued" different visions of it by often entertaining a kind of critical discussion with each other. In Chapter 6, finally, the research focuses on the way the Constitution has permeated the country's institutional life, by taking judicial discourse into account. In particular, the chapter discusses the argumentative strategies through which the Supreme Court of Ireland has exerted its jurisdiction as per Article 26 of the *Bunreacht* mentioned previously (example 16), whereby the Republic's court of last resort pronounces on the matter of the constitutionality of acts of the *Oireachtas*.

CHAPTER FIVE

BUNREACHT NA HÉIREANN IN THE PRESS: A CASE STUDY

5.1 Introduction

This chapter presents the findings of the first case study on the Constitution of Ireland in Irish public life. As we anticipated in Chapter 3, the analysis of lexical and argumentative strategies through which *Bunreacht na hÉireann* was received focuses on the *Irish Independent* and the *Irish Press*, which have been thoroughly investigated in journalism studies.

Behind the rise of the *Independent* was William Martin Murphy. The Irish businessman from Co. Cork had amassed a fortune from profitable railway investments. This enabled him to gain control of the *Irish Catholic* and the *Irish Daily Independent* in 1904, "partly as mouthpieces for his own pro-business, conservative Catholic nationalist views, but also with a view to building up a profitable media empire" (Morash 2010, 122). In doing so, evidence that Murphy was following the example set by English papers was visible from the weekend edition named *Irish Weekly Independent* appearing on Saturdays. By including special columns for farmers, women, civil servants and children, this weekly edition deliberately addressed specific readership segments. Furthermore, while reporting on the United Irish League and the Gaelic Athletic Association in favourable terms, it also carried international news.

When it was launched in 1905, the *Irish Independent* was in fact the result of the merger between the *Irish Daily Independent* and the *Daily Nation*. In recounting the history of the newspaper, Murphy (1909, 3) proclaimed that under its editorial and managerial control, the *Independent*

> will justify its claim to be a National journal, independent in fact as well as in name. It holds itself free to help on every good cause which is for Ireland's benefit. It will place our country's interests above those of party, and it will not seek to exploit any section or individual. The extravagances of partisanship will be unknown in its editorial columns. If we cannot

> always hope to reconcile disagreements in policy among public men, we shall do nothing to aggravate them. While uncompromising in its support of the demand for the restoration of the National rights of Ireland, the 'Irish Independent' will be neither offensive nor aggressive in its style of advocacy, and as a newspaper will be found acceptable by every class and creed.

The focus on an interclass readership must have been a major preoccupation for Murphy, who later in the booklet *The Story of a newspaper* reiterates the same point. For the purpose of fighting "the spirit of intolerance, which is, unfortunately, too common in Ireland", the *Independent* was expected to "bring about a different feeling amongst different classes, and promote a more cordial co-operation amongst those holding different political views in the interests of the common view of our country" (Murphy 1909, 11-12).

The man entrusted with the task of pursuing this editorial policy was the editor, T. R. Harrington, whose contribution to the *Independent*'s success is acknowledged by Larkin (2012) to have been twofold. First of all, Harrington wholeheartedly endorsed the non-partisan policy promoted by Murphy. Secondly, for the purpose of making the newspaper accessible to the busy reader of his time, he committed the *Independent* to the practice of reporting news quickly and crisply, while at the same time ensuring uncanny accuracy. His merit was therefore to kick the unfortunate habit of reporting on political meetings and public bodies through unnecessarily prolix articles. As a methodical worker, he outlined his approach by laying down the stringent guidelines journalists should adhere to in covering the 1906 general election. As Larkin (2012, 32) recalls, these were that

1. Reporters are to bear in mind the policy of the *Independent* as an impartial newspaper and are to prepare their reports in an unbiased, impartial and reliable manner.
2. They are to consider themselves representatives of the paper and not as adherents of one party or another and to approach their work with a perfectly open mind.
3. Reporters should avoid as far as possible any comments, inferences or prophesies in connection with [election] contests and confine themselves as a rule to reporting facts or speeches in a fair and impartial way, following our usual practice of not giving things fully [i.e., summarizing, rather than providing verbatim accounts].
4. It is generally advisable that reporters should engage their own cars and should come with other pressmen, if possible, and thus be independent of both the opposing parties to a contest.
5. These instructions apply to all contests anywhere in Ireland.

Immersed in the revivalist climate though it was, the *Independent*'s relationship with the Irish-Ireland movement was a complex one. On the one hand, it was no rare event for anyone to leaf through the pages of the newspaper and come across evidence that the *Indo* accepted advertisements from international companies such as Nestlé and Rowntree's (cf. Uí Fhaoláin 2014). Moreover, the *Indo* developed links with Britain at different levels. Hence, from the early stages of the Great War, the newspaper forcefully argued that "Ireland's economic and political interests lay with the empire, urged readers to enlist for overseas service and reminded them that war loans would be less costly than a German victory" (Maume 2004, 139).

Besides, tangible proof that the *Independent* saw itself as a commercial enterprise run in the context of the British Empire came from the regular inclusion of rolls of honour or 'Military Intelligence' during the War as well as ads to recommend the creation of an Irish National War Memorial, not to mention reports about imperial appointments and fashionable marriages as "daily fixtures" of the magazine "and both 'Our London Letter' and the 'Social and Personal Column'" (Whelan 2012, 78). This may not be entirely surprising, if one thinks about Murphy's own business interests in overseas railway companies.

On the other hand, there was more to the *Independent* than met the eye. For instance, Murphy played an important role in the organisation of the International Exhibition in Dublin in 1907. However, when King Edward VII as the Exhibition's patron offered him a knighthood to commend him for that, Murphy refused. Even more strikingly, no later than the very first issue did the *Independent* pledge its support "to the Irish Language and Industrial Revival Movements, as to every movement for the National and material regeneration of Ireland" (Monday, 2 January 1905). Proving the crucial point made by Uí Fhaoláin (2014, 63) as she talks about the *Independent*'s hybrid identity, it is fair to say that that the newspaper was crystal clear about its willingness to "foster the core values of nationalism, economic progress and cultural revival as promoted by the Irish-Ireland movement". Within the framework of fostering the Irish economy and Irish nationalist movements, finally, the *Independent* published articles and letters on the choice of Irish-made clothes, the undertaking of cooperative enterprises and the need to generate employment in the *Gaeltacht*. As Whelan (2012, 78) documents, the author of one of those letters went as far as to propose that a *Fáinne*-type badge should be instituted for those who preferred Irish-made clothing to imported goods.

The *Irish Press* is a more recent acquisition to the Irish media landscape. The context in which it was established in 1931 was that of post-Civil War Ireland. Nearly ten years after the Irish Free State had been proclaimed, Eamon de Valera still drew severe condemnation for not accepting the Anglo-Irish Treaty of 1921 and was blamed for the ensuing Civil War by media outlets such as the *Irish Independent* and the *Irish Times*. The latter voiced Unionist feelings, while the *Indo* was still a committed supporter of the country's Commonwealth connection. De Valera's decision to found a new newspaper should therefore also be interpreted as a reaction to such attitudes resulting in outright hostility towards him.

From a political point of view, the decade after Independence was largely dominated by *Cumann na nGaedheal*. This was the party that had ultimately taken charge of fully implementing the Treaty and had formed a strong alliance with the Catholic Church. Castigating de Valera and the whole of the anti-Treaty faction, the party could hardly appeal to the cohesiveness provided by nationalist feelings in the aftermath of the wounds inflicted by years of war, partition and sharp divisions. As a successor to the by then defunct Irish Parliamentary Party, *Cumann na nGaedheal* was to experience the difficulties of engaging in cultural politics, where it turned to religion as a shared platform of Irish nationhood (Fitzpatrick 1992). However, the party soon lost political appeal, mainly as a result of a somewhat narrow support base resting on the urban middle classes. *Cumann na nGaedheal*'s omission to shape a viable identity for the Irish people would later enable *Fianna Fáil*, the party de Valera himself launched in 1926, to exploit the country's hunger for cultural cohesiveness.

Allegedly inspired by the ideals propagating from the Irish Revival at the turn of the twentieth century, *Fianna Fáil* began as the party entrusted with the task of regenerating national consciousness in a way *Cumann na nGaedheal* had admittedly failed to do. This kind of consciousness would be both developed along the lines of language, religion, culture as well as a shared sense of history, and defined in terms of differentiation from another nation or perceived internal enemies. Against this backdrop, the *Irish Press* made a major contribution to de Valera's victory in the 1932 general election. In the years that followed, the newspaper helped establish the government's credibility and mainly acted as an organ of defence for the party, as it did in the adverse circumstances of the Spanish civil war. Notwithstanding the Catholic Church's wholehearted support for Franco, therefore, the newspaper endorsed de Valera's policy of impartiality.

De Valera kept for himself a high profile on the *Irish Press*' board as the company's controlling director. From a position that was not subject to re-election, the then *Taoiseach* took a very firm grip on the *Press* company. This was especially so because the post of controlling director "also incorporated the powerful positions of editor-in-chief and managing director", which essentially meant that de Valera "had complete control of the editorial content of the paper as well as over the appointment of all staff" (O'Brien 2001, 26).

As far as its contents were concerned, the *Irish Press* went to great lengths to popularise a concept of newsworthiness that would distinguish it from competitors. Designed to circulate across the country and be available throughout villages and crossroads, the *Irish Press* was intended to cover life in Ireland's rural environments, the Irish language (Mazzi forthcoming) and national games and pastimes. Defining itself as a newspaper that would listen to ordinary people's voice, the *Press* embraced a doctrine of social partnership. It therefore challenged the ideology of class struggle and reinforced the idea that all classes should cooperate to facilitate social and economic progress.

The *Press* actively targeted those interest groups that had not benefited from *Cumann na nGaedheal*'s economic policy in the 1920s, such as smaller farmers and businessmen, people from the urban working classes and trade unionists. As a result, the paper succeeded in "uniting a cross-class spectrum of support for Fianna Fáil's policies, the level of which was tested in the 1932 general election" (O'Brien 2001, 46). These central aspects are revealed by a number of news texts in the *Bunreacht_News* corpus as well. Thus, for instance, in a news report entitled "Look at the fruits of our work" (1 July 1937), emphasis is laid on the words of the Minister for Education in a speech delivered in Kilkenny. More specifically, in a dedicated section called "Interests of all sections", Mr O'Deirg is reported to have said that

> [w]e strongly oppose the idea that any manufacturer or industrialist is entitled to mulct the consumer; but at the same time the producer should get a fair return, so that he can give fair employment and pay decent wages. We are carrying out our policy not in the interest of one section, but in the interests of all sections.

At its inception, the *Press* appeared to advance a radical agenda. It offered a penetrating critique of Irish society as it had been shaped by the post-Independence period. Furthermore, it levelled damning criticisms in relation to issues such as the country's high unemployment rates and emigration, and it opposed what it saw as *Cumann na nGaedheal*'s submissiveness to British imperialism, as instantiated by the payment of land annuities and Ireland's ever greater economic dependence on the United Kingdom. Indeed, the promotion of protectionism and self-sufficiency (Neary and Ó Gráda 1991; Daly 1994) was to play a decisive role both in *Fianna Fáil*'s manifesto and in the *Irish Press*' stance. This can be appreciated from more than one article in *Bunreacht_News*, and chiefly in "Unity Freedom Prosperity for Whole People" published by the *Press* also on 1 July. Reporting de Valera's own words, as it very often did, the newspaper wrote as follows:

> We do want you to grow wheat and beet and the other things we need. We want the Irish workers to turn wheat into flour and to turn beet into sugar. We say to the factories that we don't want our community to have to buy clothes made outside nor do we want them to make clothes at home with cloth that is woven outside the country. We say let our weavers weave the cloth, and we go further than that if we are able, because not merely should we weave the cloth but we should spin the wool if it is possible to do it.

Despite vocal opposition from political and media opponents alike, the *Irish Press* survived and even increased its circulation after its first year of publication. In more detail, "[c]irculation rose from an average of 56,821 for the last three months of 1931 to an average of 86,825 for the second quarter of 1932, and eventually settled down at a circulation of around 90,000" (O'Brien 2001, 45). The *Irish Press*' position of prominence over the years was later testified to by the launch of its Sunday edition, known as the *Sunday Press*. By way of an innovative make-up, the issues of the *Sunday Press* were subdivided into a news section, a magazine section characterised among other things by a very appealing woman's page along with film, book and theatre reviews, and an extensive sports section. Lasting until 1995, the *Sunday Press* turned out to be "the best-selling newspaper in Ireland for one-third of the twentieth century and it was the country's foremost quality title for forty years", during which it is estimated to have reached "a total of well over 1.3 million adults each week" (Burke 2018, 79). In sum, the lifespan of and appreciation for the *Sunday Press* indicate that the *Press*' social and cultural influence was at least as significant as its political impact.

The focus of the investigation in the chapter is less on the historical background of the two newspapers than on the use of rhetorical resources through which *Irish Independent* and *Irish Press* represented and in many respects constructed the Constitution of Ireland for the respective readership. In Section 5.2, first of all, the editorial stance of the two newspapers is reviewed, while Section 5.3 looks at the way the contentious issue of women's rights was dealt with from the columns of both.

5.2 *Bunreacht na hÉireann* in news columns: Lexis and argumentation in the *Irish Independent* and the *Irish Press*

As we are well aware, the news texts from which newspapers' stance is more obviously stressed are editorials. It is therefore from such texts that this first strand of the analysis will begin. In particular, two editorials can be said to be outstanding in that they embed the real substance of the two newspapers' views on *Bunreacht na hÉireann*, not to mention that they literally read as a response to each other.

The first text is an editorial published by the *Irish Independent* on 29 December with the headline "The Constitution". In the opening paragraph, the writer clearly alludes to an unspecified text published by the *Irish Press*, sarcastically referred to as *the tied newspaper, which has to praise every act of the Fianna Fáil party*. The *Press*, it is reported, described the Constitution as a *"complete charter of nationhood"*, a claim the rest of the editorial is devoted to disproving. The core of the *Independent*'s argumentation lies in the passage reported below as (1):[1]

(1) Nobody will be deceived by this *raiméis*. Not one jot or little or additional liberty is secured to any citizen. In fact, it is all the other way about; for the new Constitution contains clauses which may possibly be used to interfere with freedom of speech, freedom of the Press, with freedom of associations, and the rights of women. The Constitution has imposed upon the public the new and costly office of President with powers which the titular head of a democratic State should not be given. It has established a new Seanad which is at least as unsatisfactory in the method of election as its predecessor was. The sad part of this business is that it would have been possible to amend the Constitution so as to have it an agreed measure. But Mr de Valera's vanity and obstinacy were proof against reason. [...] This "complete charter of nationhood" had a majority of only 158,160, or one eleventh of the electorate. More than 526,000 votes were cast against it: very much less than half of the electorate voted in favour of it. In no democratic country would a Constitution be carried on such figures. It is impossible for the people to have for this Constitution the respect that would rightly be accorded to one adopted with the deliberation and dignity required for such an instrument.

---

[1] Unless expressly mentioned in the running text of the chapter, the headline of the news texts the examples are taken from is reported in brackets. In addition, all emphasis, wherever present, is mine.

In what reads as a stinging indictment of the Constitution, the standpoint (S) is unmistakably that Ireland's new fundamental law is flawed and commands no respect. In an instance of multiple argumentation, the standpoint is supported by two independent argument schemes. The first is symptomatic argumentation, while the second is causal argumentation. With the former, a symptomatic relationship is established between the defining traits of the Constitution and its lack of democratic credentials. As can be seen from the schematisation proposed below, first and foremost, the Constitution's flaws are its tendency to interfere with fundamental freedoms such as that of speech, the press and associations (A), to award the President enormous powers (B) and to provide for the formation of a second chamber on a fully unsatisfactory basis (C). Moreover, it is argued, the Constitution lacks the legitimacy that a document of its kind should enjoy, because it was endorsed by *only 158,160* votes, *or one-eleventh of the electorate* (D).

In order to make the symptomatic argument more cogent, the readers' attention is drawn to Ireland as a somewhat special case, since *in no democratic country would a Constitution be carried on such figures*. Interestingly, the echo of this formulation reverberates in other editorials of the corpus, such as that published on 8 July ("The Constitution"). Here, the writer similarly states that *in no other country could so far-reaching a change* as that envisioned by the *Bunreacht be brought about by a minority vote.* In (2) below, Y is the property of "being flawed", X is the Constitution and A, B, C and D are the traits we isolated earlier on:

(2) Y is true of X
because A, B, C and D are true of X
and A, B, C and D go characteristically with Y

In association with the symptomatic argumentation, a powerful causal argument is put forward. In this case, a causal link is established between de Valera's attitude (*vanity and obstinacy*) and the fact that the Constitution is no agreed document, since a number of overdue amendments were not even taken into account. From a linguistic point of view, the correlation between the use of third-conditional structures (e.g., *it would have been possible to amend the Constitution…*) and causality has been demonstrated (Nivelle and Van Belle 2007; Mazzi 2010). Here, by rephrasing the sentence quoted before, the schematisation in (3) can be suggested:

(3) Mr. de Valera was vain and obstinate.
→ It was not possible to amend the Constitution as required.
→ The Constitution is no agreed document.
→ The Constitution is flawed.

Overall, therefore, the structure of the *Independent*'s argumentation can be reproduced as in Figure 5.1. This kind of argumentation is representative of the *Indo*'s view of the new charter introduced in 1937. As such, it is articulated in the other editorials included in the corpus, which attaches further importance to the schematisation below:

Figure 5.1. Argument structure behind the *Irish Independent*'s stance on the Constitution.

S: The Constitution is flawed and commands no respect.

Symptomatic Argumentation Causal Argumentation

The response from the *Irish Press* duly came the day after (30 December), where it materialised through the editorial "Campaign against the Constitution". The text begins by immediately targeting its competitor, accused of dealing with *Bunreacht na hÉireann* through statements "of such an extraordinary character" they cannot be glossed over in silence, because they "would seem to foreshadow a deliberate campaign of *sabotage* directed against the new charter with which Eire has endowed herself". In order to support the standpoint (S) that the Constitution marks a historical turning point for Ireland and to discredit the *Independent*, the *Press* puts forward two independent argument schemes. The former is undoubtedly an instance of *ad hominem* designed to undermine the *Independent*'s credibility, as shown by (4):

(4) On what grounds has this paper with its record in Easter Week when even the agents of British rule could not satisfy its blood lust, the authority to proclaim that the new Constitution was undeserving of respect and should be treated accordingly?

The *Press* cunningly reminds readers of the *Indo*'s hostile reaction to the Easter Rising, when the newspaper was very critical towards the insurgents. In other words, the *Independent* is portrayed as a quintessentially anti-national publication, whose words about the putative lack of respectability of the Constitution ought to be rejected accordingly. In line with the formalisation of direct *ad hominem* arguments in Walton (2010,

8), the *Press*' argument could be schematized as in Figure 5.2, where A is of course the *Independent* itself:

Figure 5.2. Argumentation *ad hominem* in the *Irish Press*.

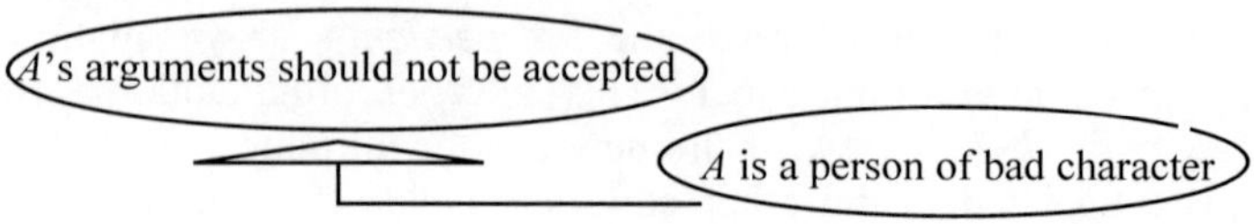

Along with the argumentation *ad hominem*, the editorial avails itself of a fairly articulated symptomatic argument illustrated in (5):

> (5) Is it not a fact that the Fine Gael Party were invited to take their part in framing the instrument, but they declined to avail of the opportunity of making their contribution to its preparation which was presented to them? When introduced in the Dáil in legislative form was not every effort made to have it treated as being a non-party and non-controversial measure which would affect the whole future of the nation and which was superior to party interests and passing political differences? […] When every proposal for dealing with the question from the broadest national standpoint had been flung back in the face of the Government, it was passed by the Dáil in the ordinary course, and following the normal procedure, but every fair-minded man will admit that the discussions in Committee were conducted in a tolerant and becoming spirit, that every point raised was duly considered […]. It was then submitted to a national plebiscite. We need not now go into the manner in which it was travestied, caricatured and misrepresented, but the fact remains that it secured national endorsement and is now the instrument which will guide and govern the future destiny of this nation.

Briefly, the Constitution is sound in that cooperation from the opposition was sought and the charter was never discussed as a party-political issue (A), every point raised in relation to it was given due consideration (*...discussions […] were conducted in a tolerant and becoming spirit...*) (B), and the *Bunreacht* received *national endorsement* (C). It is noteworthy that the writer's argumentation is linguistically reinforced by the use of rhetorical questions–see *is it not...?*; *was not every effort made...?*–and formulations that depict otherwise controversial claims, to say the least, as if they were undisputed truths–e.g. *is it not a fact that...*; *but every fair-minded man will admit that...* and *the fact remains that...* In the schematisation in (6) below, Y is the property of "being worth guiding the nation's destiny" and X is again "the Irish Constitution":

(6) Y is true of X
because A, B and C are true of X
and A, B and C go characteristically with Y

The overall structure of the *Press*' argumentation can therefore be read as in Figure 5.3:

Figure 5.3. Argument structure behind the *Irish Press*' stance on the Constitution.

S: The Constitution marks a historical turning point for Ireland.

Ad hominem argumentation Symptomatic argumentation

The relative strength of this kind of argument structure can be found elsewhere in the corpus, where it appears to be boosted through three main kinds of rhetorical resources. The first is a somewhat sensationalist approach to the people's reaction to the enactment of the Constitution. The second is the editor's choice to put voices from the Catholic Church in a prominent place. And the third is the deliberate attempt to compare the new document with the old Free State Constitution adopted soon after Independence. These resources are documented in the rest of this section.

To begin with, what tells news narratives from the *Irish Press* apart from the *Independent* is that the *Press* tends to represent the Constitution and its reception by the general public much more triumphantly even in news reports. Unlike in the *Indo*, where the tone of articles definitely tends to be matter-of-fact, the sensationalism of reporters from the *Press* could hardly go unnoticed. A comparative look at the following excerpts from the two newspapers will help clarify the point. In (7) and (8), on the one hand, the writers' language draws heavily on both impersonality and hedging (*it is believed*; *would in all probability*; *suggestions have been made*; *so far as I can gather*; *it seems certain that*) for the purpose of projecting a well-balanced picture of the likely developments in the legislative arena:

(7) Article 62 of the Constitution provides that the Government may take action by resolution in the Dáil to have the Constitution become law in a lesser period than six months. Such action by the Government, it is believed, would in all probability meet with an adverse vote in the House. [...] In view of the heavy adverse vote against the Constitution–the vote was for 686,942, against 528,296–a sharp division of opinion in the Dáil on the question of its early enactment is something, which it is believed the Government will desire to avoid. [...] Suggestions have been made, in view of the

heavy vote against the Constitution, that it should be amended within the next six months in respect of those features which produced the opposition. So far as I can gather, the Government do not propose to introduce any amendments, at least so soon. ("The draft Constitution–Government probable tactics")

(8) ...any decision as to whether the name Eire will be recognised officially would be premature before the Constitution actually came into being. Very shortly, however, it seems certain that a decision will be announced on the question whether the British Government will accept Eire as the name of the Free State, or continue to call it the Free State, or find some other alternative. ("Britain's attitude")

On the other hand, only in a minority of cases is the dominant tone in the *Press*' reports on the neutral side. To be more precise, the lexical choices attested across the news texts provide evidence that the Constitution is mainly represented through items from four lexical fields, i.e. "grandeur and pageantry", "history in the making", "suitability to the event" and "health". As regards the first, on many occasions do words and phrases in news reports reflect the *Press*' own attempts to extol the virtues of the Constitution, by focusing on the people's allegedly jubilant mood upon the document's enactment as well as their large numbers (examples 9-11). Then, *Press* reporters duly emphasise that the charter coming into force is not merely a legal text, but rather a watershed in Ireland's history (12 and 13). Furthermore, writers stubbornly insist that the monumental scale of celebrations is only suitable to the event of the new charter acquiring legal force (14). Finally, there are passages where the *Bunreacht* is depicted as a remedy to the constitutional ills the country used to suffer from (15):

(9) **The Constitution was hailed** in Bantry **with great rejoicing. Flags were flown from many houses** and patriotic mottoes spanned the principal streets. Tar barrels were lighted during the evening, and **large crowds gathered** around them **and** sang patriotic songs and **cheered the Constitution**. [...] **Large numbers** went from Mallow and surrounding districts at night to a public demonstration in Kanturk [...]. ("Crowds gather to cheer the Constitution")

(10) **Constitution Day was hailed with jubilation** in all parts of Eire. There was **a great display of Tricolours**; **banners** bearing patriotic mottoes **spanned the streets of many towns**; bonfires blazed last night from the hill-tops around Dublin, Tipperary, Wexford [...] and in Co. Cork **large crowds gathered** around burning tar barrels **to**

sing the National Anthem fervently and **cheer** the coming of the new enactment. ("How country welcomed Constitution")

(11) At night **a large bonfire** was lighted amid **the cheers of a large crowd** which congregated on the Fair Green […]. ("Demonstration around huge bonfire")

(12) The crews stood to their guns, the artillery officer waiting for the stroke of the half-hour when another great shot was to be **fired into history**. […] As one iron mouth after another opened with a roar, the thunderous and prolonged salute shook the quiet fields and boomed through the city–**salute to destiny that echoed** not only through the streets of its capital, but from shore to shore of this island–triumphant salvo that **will echo down the years**. ("Dublin's day of pageantry")

(13) The old people used to talk with pride about the meetings addressed by O'Connell, which they attended, and **in years to come** the children of to-day would tell that they attended the Mass for the new Constitution. ("Ireland's Constitution now in force")

(14) New era to be **fittingly** opened–On Wednesday next–Lá an Bhunreachta–the new Constitution of Eire will come into force. There will be **suitable** religious and military ceremony throughout the State. ("Constitution Day")

(15) This was not a political but **a natural Constitution**. […] It would act as **a medium for healing** the divisions and splits that had taken place in the past. ("Demonstration around huge bonfire")

In examples (9)-(11), one's attention is drawn to the frequent use of the adjective *large* along with verbs such as *hail* and *cheer*, while the use of the words *history* and *years* in context suggests that the memory of the new Constitution's enactment will indeed be a long-lasting one. Moreover, the idea that only grandiose plans would be suited to receive news of the enactment, as well as the notion of the new charter as a remedy against the evils marring the country over previous years (e.g. the Civil War) seem particularly forceful in reinforcing the *Irish Press*' stance documented earlier on.

In second place, there is strong evidence that the *Irish Press* is much more prone than the *Irish Independent* to reporting the Catholic Church's favourable opinion of the Constitution. This trend, which can be identified as being largely instrumental in heightening the impression that the charter is indeed a good document, emerges in two ways. The first lies in reporting the words of influential members from the Hierarchy, whereas the second is the habit of reviewing the Catholic press from around the world, from the United Kingdom to Australia and, of course, the Vatican itself. In both cases, the presence of symptomatic argumentation can be detected.

As for the Hierarchy's voice, most of the reported statements stress that the Preamble to the Constitution recognises God as the source from which power is derived (cf. Section 1.6). In addition, there are statements that the charter embodies Christian principles as a bedrock on which Irish society is based. Finally, the Constitution is presented as a document emanating from a truly Catholic leader (notably, de Valera) ruling over a quintessentially Catholic people. These three aspects, which shall be referred to as A, B and C, are highlighted in examples (16) and (17).

(16) The Bishop of Kildare and Leighlin, Most Rev. Dr. Keogh, preaching in Carlow Cathedral, said he wished to refer to the new Constitution. [...] "The Constitution **is unique because on the front page it is acknowledged that God is the source from which all ruling power is derived**, and the new Constitution **is based on the big broad principles which alone can give security to society**". ("Carlow Cathedral Mass")

(17) We have been requested to publish the following letter, which expresses the views of a number of leading Irish priests [...] "If such an occasion as the coming into existence of a Constitution such as ours, and **a fundamental statement from the Leader of a Catholic people, penned by a Catholic Leader**, came from the Leader of any other country, the Church bells of that nation would ring out exultingly, and that nation would go on its knees to thank its God". ("Leading priests' letter")

In the two passages, the speakers–respectively, the Bishop of Kildare and Leighlin, and a group of leading Irish priests–establish a symptomatic relationship between the above features and the notion that the *Bunreacht* is a major political breakthrough for Ireland, as in the schematisation in (18) below. Here, Y is the property of "being a major political breakthrough", while X is the Constitution:

(18) Y is true of X
because A, B and C are true of X
and A, B and C go characteristically with Y

The views conveyed in (16) and (17) are symptomatic of the truly radical rhetoric underlying the Catholic Church's posture in Irish public life at the time. This can be appreciated from other news texts as well, such as a letter from a Dominican preacher that is full of words and phrases from the lexical field of "war". Thus, he maintains, the Constitution has the merit of including provisions such as Article 43 against "the dissolution of marriage". These norms should be part of the Church's strong reaction to the "efforts" made "both publicly and privately" "to combat the morality taught by the Church" as well as the "warfare" directed "against the family and the Christian home" to "shake the stability of the divine institution of marriage".

On the one hand, it is clear that the responsibility for the statements in (16) and (17) does not immediately lie with the *Irish Press*. Besides, the words of prominent members of the clergy are also reported in news texts published by the *Independent*. On the other hand, the frequency with which the *Press* featured them in its daily columns may suggest that either the newspaper broadly shared them, or it used them to persuasively back up its own stance on the Constitution.

After all, indicating that one's position was supported by the Church would tick all the right boxes at the time. As a matter of fact, the dominant position of the Catholic Church in 1930s Ireland was beyond dispute, suffice it to think of the International Eucharistic Congress. This was a landmark event for Irish Catholicism, which took place in Dublin precisely in 1932, marking the 1500th anniversary of St. Patrick's arrival on Irish soil. It turned out to be an overwhelmingly popular event, with about 100,000 children attending the Special Children's Mass on 25 June, 200,000 women attending the Women's Mass on 24 June, 250,000 men present at the Men's Mass of 23 June, and approximately one million people attending the Final Mass held at Phoenix Park, "an extraordinary number for a sparsely populated country" (Holmes 2000, 68).

The logic behind the inclusion of lengthy reviews from influential Catholic papers from around the world can be observed to be the same. While the *Independent* section of the corpus comprises no such texts, their presence across the issues of the *Irish Press* is conspicuous. More specifically, the *Press* published reviews from the *Catholic Herald* (England), *The Holy Name Monthly* (Australia and New Zealand), *La Civiltà Cattolica* as well as the *Osservatore Romano* (Italy/the Vatican) and *The Cross* (Irish edition). In these periodicals, symptomatic argumentation is again the predominant type of rhetorical strategy. In the main, the symptomatic relationship is between the property of displaying "the principles outlined by the Popes" ("An Australian appreciation–

Catholic monthly reviews new Constitution"), those "of the Christian doctrine" of the State ("'More than a milestone'–Vatican organ tribute to new Constitution"), a "profoundly Christian character" as well as "consonance with the teaching of the Church and with the Papal Encyclicals on Social Justice" ("'Profoundly Christian Character'–Passionist Fathers' magazine on the new Constitution"), and the standpoint that the *Bunreacht* is more than a milestone and in fact the means through which Ireland will fulfil the national aspirations for which she fought for years. In other words, it is the Papal nature of the charter, so to speak, that motivates its positive reception from a Catholic point of view.

Finally, the *Press* boosts the strength of its argumentation by comparing the benefits of the new Constitution with the putative downsides of the old Free State Constitution in force between 1922 and 1937 (Lee 1989). In various news reports, the standpoint that the new Constitution should be welcomed as a substantial improvement to the State's political infrastructure is supported by two interrelated argument schemes. The first is pragmatic argumentation in its first variant. In this case, the action of endorsing the new constitutional project is called for on the grounds that it will produce highly desirable outcomes: among these, proper recognition for "the Glory of God and the Honour of Ireland" ("President's powers–Dr. Ryan on 'unholy alliance' against Constitution"), restoring the dignity of the Irish language, acknowledging that Ireland's sovereignty resides in the whole of the 32 counties rather than the 26 of the Free State, and the fact that the country's destiny is in the safe hands of the Irish people instead of depending on an alien government's approval. These achievements are presented as having been made possible by *Bunreacht na hÉireann*, while the old Free State Constitution purportedly stood in the way of such concrete steps, as can be seen from examples (19) and (20) below:

(19) Article 2 declares the national territory consists of the whole island of Ireland, its islands and territorial seas. **There was no corresponding article in the old Constitution** but reference was made to "the area of jurisdiction of the Irish Free State at the time of the coming into action of this Constitution". [...] As to the Irish language, **the old Constitution** declared it to be the National language, but **specified that the English language should be equally recognised. The new Constitution specifies that Irish** as the National language **"is the first official language"**. English is given second place. ("Old and new compared")

(20) The old Constitution was brought into existence in 1922. The then Provisional Government appointed a Committee in February of that year and **a draft Constitution was prepared and submitted for**

approval as required by the British Government. The present Constitution was, of course, **submitted to no authority outside Ireland**. ("Put to people on day of poll: The 1922 provisions–And England had previously to approve!")

In a prime example of coordinative argumentation, the *Irish Press*' pragmatic argument is joined with a causal argument lying in a number of articles that are actually lengthy verbatim reports of de Valera's speeches in favour of the Constitution he actively shaped. In these texts, the *Taoiseach* forcefully asserts that rejecting the new Constitution would ultimately result in *leaving things as they are*, and therefore opting for an old Constitution he describes as *a badge of subjection on our people* (example 21). The only way to break the causal chain, de Valera's argument goes, is to choose *Bunreacht na hÉireann*:

(21) "Those who opposed the Constitution wanted the people to leave things as they are. […] Those who are asking you not to vote for the Constitution–I don't care where they are–whether on the right or on the left–whether they are women or men–they are asking you, the Irish people, to take in preference to an Irish document–a document that was made by outsiders and which is, as long as it remains, a badge of subjection on our people". ("Unity Freedom Prosperity for whole people")

The overall argument structure behind the comparison between the two constitutions can therefore be schematised as in Figure 5.4 below:

Figure 5.4. Argument structure behind the *Irish Press*' comparison of old and new Constitution.

S: The new Constitution should be welcomed as a substantial improvement on the old.

Pragmatic argumentation ⟷ Causal argumentation

Pragmatic argumentation	Causal argumentation
1. Action X [endorsing *Bunreacht na hÉireann*] should be performed. 1.1a Action X leads to W, Y, Z etc. [extending the country's sovereignty, restoring the centrality of the Irish language etc.] 1.1b W, Y, Z etc. are desirable 1.1a-1.1b' (If Action Z leads to W, Y, Z etc. and W, Y, Z etc. are desirable, then Action X should be performed)	You do not vote for the new Constitution. ↓ You want to leave things as they are. ↓ You are happy with the country being subjugated by Britain.

The last part of this section shows the rich repertoire of rhetorical resources mobilised by the *Irish Press* in its relentless effort to promote the new Constitution. The qualitative analysis of the corpus texts, however, does more than simply shed light on the two newspapers' political alignment *vis-à-vis* the new charter. It also provides evidence of a wider social debate over the *Bunreacht* in relation to the topical issue of the conceptualisation of the role of women in Irish society. This is the object of the next section.

5.3 *Bunreacht na hÉireann* and Irish women in the press

The main reason why the role of women in the Constitution deserves to be elucidated is that this issue offers a fine example of how newspapers may serve as *fora* for public representatives and the citizenship to discuss matters of high social impact. In relation to women's figure across the 1937 issues of the two newspapers instantiated in the corpus, what is most striking is less their stance *per se* than the way a range of social actors, so to speak, used newspapers to enter a meaningful dialogue by interacting with and responding to one another.

To begin with, the debate focuses on Article 40, where it is provided that "[a]ll citizens shall, as human persons, be held equal before the law. This shall not be held to mean that the State shall not in its enactments have due regard to differences of capacity, physical and moral, and of social function". From the pages of the *Irish Press* of 6 December, on the one hand, the Minister for Agriculture brings his own perspective on the views for which the promoters of *Bunreacht na hÉireann* (*they* in example 22) came under attack. In his opinion, the above norm should be interpreted as meaning that the State will not force anyone–including women–to do work that does not fit their profile. In what is explicitly presented as "a reply to a speech made recently at Glynn, Co. Wexford, by Dr Ryan, Minister for Agriculture" (*Irish Independent*, 16 December), on the other hand, Professor Mary Hayden (Emergency Committee of the National University Women Graduates' Association) estimates the obnoxious effects Article 40 might have for women (23):

(22) "They were attacked because they said the State must not force people to do work unsuited to their sex, age, or strength". ("President's powers–Dr. Ryan on 'unholy alliance' against Constitution")

(23) It would be quite possible, in accordance with this Article, to forbid the employment of women in any particular industry, or their entrance

> into any particular profession. […] Already we have grown accustomed to read in the daily papers advertisements from Government departments inviting applications for posts–legal, medical, musical, etc., in which, while equal qualifications are required from female and male applicants, the salary offered to the one (married or unmarried) exceeds by sometimes more than a third that to be given to the other. Yet we are told that women are not differentiated against! ("Critics of the Constitution–A salaries' point")

It follows from a comparison of the two passages that the Minister interprets Article 40 as having a liberal concept, whereas Prof Hayden skilfully combines the second variant of pragmatic argumentation with a fairly straightforward example. The new Constitution, so the argument goes, should not be accepted on the grounds that it would lead to harmful consequences, namely preventing women from being employed in a number of sectors. Moreover, there is evidence that discrimination is already being practiced, because Government departments themselves have been advertising jobs for which a serious imbalance is created between male and female applicants at a salary level.

Remarkably, this exchange of opinions was not to spell the end of the controversy. In the article "Attacks on Constitution–Dr. Ryan replies to women critics" published by the *Indo*, Rev. Murphy, Dr Ryan's host, dismissed Prof Hayden's line of argument by essentially discrediting women and reducing dissent from the Constitution to them as a bunch of *noisy* people (example 24). In turn, the reply to Rev. Murphy's stinging attack came two days later in the form of a letter to the editor of the *Independent*. Interestingly, the letter is signed as "Amazed", and it gives the figures of the popular vote against the Constitution: as we saw in (7) earlier on, this amounted to more than half a million votes, a number the cryptic writer of the letter sarcastically doubts can refer to a population of *noisy women* alone (25):

(24) Rev. P. Murphy, Glyan, who presided, paid a tribute to Dr. Ryan, who, he said, was a Minister of the most Catholic Government in the world. The opposition to the new Constitution, he added, came mainly from a number of noisy women […]. ("Attacks on Constitution–Dr. Ryan replies to women critics")

(25) In Monday's *Irish Independent*, Rev. P. Murphy […] is reported as saying: "The opposition to the Constitution came mainly from a number of noisy women […]". As 526,945 votes were cast against

> the Constitution, we must possess an astounding population of noisy women […]. ("The Constitution")

More generally, the tendency to undermine women's credentials as legitimate stakeholders in the debate is pronounced. Thus, for instance, the article "Westmeath T.D.'s call" (*Irish Press*, 30 December) reports the words of TD M. J. Kennedy at a meeting in Castlepollard, where he exposed women as being only motivated by "hatred of Eamon de Valera, hatred of Fianna Fáil, and hatred of the constitution of the Irish home where the bean a thighe was respected and enthroned". Unlike in their gloomy predictions on the eve of Constitution Day, Mr Kennedy pointed out, "women had not lost their positions nor ceased to follow their professions. Their names were still on the voters' lists with the same rights as men".

Moreover, trenchant criticism against women came from the Vice-President of the Executive Council, Sean T. O'Kelly. Talking about anti-Constitution propaganda at a meeting at Wynn's Hotel, Dublin, Mr O'Kelly belittled women who were critical of *Bunreacht na hÉireann* as people who had contributed to the national cause in no meaningful way and would rather keep living *under the Union Jack*. In a rather astute move designed to take full advantage of symptomatic argumentation, women are essentially depicted as utterly anti-national, an attitude that characteristically entails lack of trustworthiness (example 26).

Two days later (16 December), Mary J. Hogan, Hon. Sec. of the Emergency Committee of the National University Women Graduates' Association, addressed a letter to the editor of the *Irish Press* to fight back. In Ms Hogan's letter, Mr O'Kelly's symptomatic argumentation is reversed. In her opinion, Irish women have a track record proving their direct involvement in the struggle for Irish nationality. Indeed, one example provided by the writer is telling: this is Mrs Denis McCullough, sister of Dr Ryan and sister-in-law of O'Kelly himself, who along with others testified to women's active and voluntary participation even *in the arduous days of 1916 and subsequent years*. Their contribution, the argument goes, is indicative of their right to have their say on the constitutional architecture of the new State (27):

(26) Mr. O'Kelly, replying, said that they had triumphed over all propaganda brought to bear against the Constitution. There had been terrific misrepresentations of the document. One line of attack that he thought was most successful, was the attack which misrepresented the position of women under the Constitution. Many women were mislead [sic]: but those responsible for the propaganda **had never**

done anything for the cause of Irish independence, and would rather see the country still under the Union Jack. ("Minister and Constitution–Aims outlined; history traced")

(27) The further indictment of the organisers as having a poor national record shows a strange ignorance of recent Irish history. We have only to mention such names as Dr. Kathleen Lynn, Hannah Sheehy-Skeffington, Geraldine Plunkett-Dillon (sister of Joseph Plunkett), Mrs. Denis McCullough (sister of Dr. Ryan and sister-in-law of Mr. Sean T. O'Kelly), Sheila Bowen-Dowling, and Eileen Davitt (carrying on the tradition of her noble father), **to give the lie to any insinuation that the women on the platform had failed to give any account of themselves in the arduous days of 1916 and subsequent years.** ("Women and the Constitution")

Whether on behalf of the two newspapers (Section 5.2), or in the name of public figures as well as members of the citizenship (Section 5.3), news texts offer a vivid account of the function of media outlets as a vehicle of lively debate in Ireland's public sphere in the year of the new Constitution. This aspect is further explored in the last section of the chapter.

5.4 Conclusions

The findings presented in this chapter provide us with a comprehensive overview of the way two leading newspapers of the age performed their role of knowledge disseminators in the Irish public sphere. The data reviewed across Sections 5.2 and 5.3 should not of course be taken as evidence of the fact that *Bunreacht na hÉireann* was merely discussed from party-political or in any case multiple perspectives, and was therefore hardly ever subject to rigorous examination in the press. Quite the opposite, the corpus also includes highly informative news reports that provide access to the contents of the new charter, especially in the *Irish Independent*. These texts tell readers about the scope of key constitutional norms such as those regarding the President's powers and the number of government ministers (example 28); they review the measures through which the Constitution is implemented (29); and they direct readers to forthcoming materials they should consider perusing in order to know more about the charter (30):

(28) Legislation passed by the Oireachtas shall be signed by the President not earlier than five days nor later than seven days after it has been presented for signature. [...]. The Government will consist of not

fewer than seven and not more than 15 members. Not more than two may be senators. ("The King recognised")

(29) Five new Bills implementing the Constitution are being introduced tomorrow. They are: Interpretation Bill 1937, which is intended "to make, for the purpose of the Constitution of Ireland lately enacted by the people, divers [sic] provisions in relation to the form, operation, and interpretation of the Acts of the Oireachtas and of instruments made under such Acts". ("Five new Bills")

(30) The "Sunday Independent" will be published as usual next Sunday. Its numerous special features will include a detailed examination and explanation of the new Constitution coming into operation next Wednesday. Written in simple and direct language by a legal expert who has made a close study of the Bunreacht, the article provides an invaluable analysis, which readers would be well advised to peruse and to keep for future reference as a comprehensive yet concise guide. ("Analysis of new Constitution–Invaluable guide")

Having said that, what is most apparent in both *Irish Independent* and *Irish Press* is the use of news discourse in order to affect and at once reflect public perception of the historic document due to come into operation in late 1937. In the attempt to affect the average reader's perception of the document, first of all, the two newspapers take differing viewpoints in relation to the innovations brought by Ireland's new fundamental law. On the one hand, the *Independent* voices its scepticism over both the substance of the *Bunreacht*–e.g. the powers of the new President–and the method chosen to adopt it, namely a plebiscite in favour of the Constitution by a very narrow margin. On the other hand, due to its capacity as a sounding board for *Fianna Fáil*, the *Irish Press*' adherence to the constitutional project envisaged by de Valera is beyond question.

What is noteworthy, secondly, is that the *Press*' propaganda machine, as it were, appears to work through a more extensive repertoire of rhetorical devices. Not only, therefore, do editorials extol the virtues of the Constitution, but the newspaper's praise of the charter also includes a somewhat more biased coverage of Constitution Day, as many people celebrated the *Bunreacht* coming into force. In addition, strong emphasis is laid on the Catholic Church's alignment with the principles behind the Constitution in the form of both statements from members of the Hierarchy and favourable comments from Catholic periodicals at home and abroad. Finally, the *Press* corroborates its views by favourably comparing the new Constitution with the old. This last strategy must have proven particularly effective because of the stigma attached by many to the Irish Free State Constitution as a symbol of unaccomplished freedom. In the eyes of several contemporary readers, the comparative advantages brought by the *Bunreacht* as opposed to its predecessor and other fundamental laws such as the American Constitution (cf. "Tribute to Bunreacht na hÉireann–American Minister's anniversary talk on Constitution of U.S.", 18 September) must have outweighed the disadvantage of the mildly unsatisfactory outcome of the plebiscite.

As regards the use of news discourse for the purpose of reflecting public perception of the new Constitution, a most controversial issue dominating the pages of the two newspapers was observed to be the construction of women's role in Irish society as of the *Bunreacht* itself. For a number of articles and letters to the editor addressing and responding to one another, the analysis of argumentative discourse carried out in the chapter was extended to the opinions exchanged by public figures such as government ministers and women's representatives, the newspapers' own position on the matter somehow slipping into the background. The rich diversity of perspectives on the status of women as well as the Constitution at large, and the very fact that competing voices join in critical discussion with often overlapping strategies yet different commitments provide evidence of a livelier public discourse in 1930s Ireland than might have been expected. This may at least indicate that, 15 years after Independence, Irish journalism had actually achieved the ambition of contributing to a society characterised by an increased civic conscience.

This chapter has investigated the relationship between the Constitution and Irish society at the level of public discourse represented by the press. In the next chapter, the focus will shift to the impact of constitutional norms at a higher level, namely by looking at *Bunreacht na hÉireann* as the yardstick by which to assess the acceptability of Acts of the *Oireachtas*. In particular, the analysis will focus on the argumentative discourse in the 15 judgments delivered by the Supreme Court under Article 26 of the Constitution. The chapter will therefore assess whether there is a degree of consistency in the argument schemes chosen by Irish Justices as they decide on the compatibility of Acts with the letter of the country's fundamental law.

CHAPTER SIX

THE CONSTITUTION AND THE JUDICIARY: A CASE STUDY ON ARGUMENTATION IN THE SUPREME COURT

6.1 Introduction

In Chapter 5, the Constitution's reception by the Irish people was discussed through the lens of national news media. It is the purpose of this chapter to explore the relationship between *Bunreacht na hÉireann* and the Irish public sphere at a specialised level. A case study is therefore undertaken on the impact of the Republic's fundamental law on the judiciary. In particular, the Supreme Court of Ireland's (SCI) argumentation is examined in the context of Article 26 references. Under this article, the Irish President is entitled to refer a bill to the Supreme Court for a decision on its constitutionality.

Should the President decide that a test on constitutional validity is required, s/he has to consult with the Council of State. This includes the *Taoiseach*, *Tánaiste* [Deputy Prime Minister], Chief Justice, President of the High Court, the Chairs of both *Dáil* and *Seanad*, the Attorney General and any of the former Presidents, *Taoisigh* or Chief Justices willing to serve, along with a number of presidential nominees up to seven (Elgie and Fitzgerald 2005, 308). It is important to note that the Council's role, in this as well as any other matter on which the President addresses it, is essentially advisory in that the President is not requested to accept its recommendations. In addition, the President's power to submit bills to the Supreme Court is limited by the Constitution. Hence, legislation relating to the public finances as certified by the Chairman of *Dáil Éireann* (see example 13 from Chapter 4), bills bringing forward proposals to amend the Constitution and bills rushed through the *Seanad* as "urgent and immediately necessary for the preservation of the public peace and security, or by reason of a public emergency" (Article 24.1) may not be referred.

Bills are not signed into law until the Court has taken its decision. Then, if the Court pronounces in favour of the constitutionality of a bill, the President has to sign it. If, on the other hand, the SCI considers any provision of the bill to be repugnant to the Constitution, the President must not sign it. The crucial aspect inherent in Article 26 is that it triggers a mechanism by which to obtain an advance ruling on the constitutionality of proposed legislation. As Byrne et al. (2014, 573) argue, this

> can be a matter of some importance where the constitutionality of a proposed law has been questioned or where it is constitutionally or politically desirable to clarify doubts in advance of its being implemented. While the power has been exercised a number of times by different Presidents it is generally believed that it is better that it is used sparingly, given its associated difficulties.

The main "associated difficulties" identified by Casey (2000) and Byrne et al. (2014) include the fact that invalidity of even a minor provision in a bill will eventually defeat it in its entirety as well as the immunity from further challenge conferred on bills by their passing judicial scrutiny. As specified in Article 34.3.3, for bills referred to the SCI and whose constitutionality has been upheld by the Court, "no Court whatever shall have jurisdiction to question the validity of a law, or any provision of a law". Since the Constitution was enacted, Presidents have referred a total of 15 bills to the Supreme Court. Eight of these have been declared constitutional, while seven have been pronounced repugnant to the Constitution in whole or in part.

The role of Article 26 in Irish constitutional life, as it were, is a strong motivation behind this chapter, too. In Section 6.2, first of all, the prototypical structure of Article 26 judgments is reviewed, in order to get readers to familiarise themselves with their overall textual organisation. In Section 6.3, then, the findings from the qualitative case study of argumentative discourse in the 15 judgments of the *SCI_26* corpus are presented. As we will see, data show that pragmatic argumentation lies at the heart of the Supreme Court's discourse. More specifically (Subsections 6.3.1 and 6.3.2), the analysis provides evidence of what variants of the argument scheme appear most closely correlated with the Court's discourse and embedded in the patterns of complex argumentation elucidated by Feteris (2016) (cf. Chapter 2, Subsection 2.5.2). In Sections 6.2. and 6.3, a more limited amount of cases was taken into account, both because of their centrality to Irish society and for the purpose of illustrating the findings with more clarity and detail.

6.2 Article 26 judgments: Textual structure

A manual reading of Article 26 judgments reveals a highly standardised text structure, which is explored in this section by looking at the SCI's decision in the matter of the Regulation of Information (Services outside the State for Termination of Pregnancies) Bill, 1995 [S.C. No. 87 of 1995]. The long title of the bill concerned was as follows: "An Act to prescribe the conditions subject to which certain information relating to services lawfully available outside the State for the termination of pregnancies and to persons who provide such services may be given to individual women or the general public, to amend the Indecent Advertisements Act, 1889, and the Censorship of Publications Acts, 1929 to 1967, and to provide for related matters".

As discussed elsewhere (Mazzi 2016), abortion was a controversial issue in Ireland for a very long time, at least until a referendum repealed the Eighth Amendment of the Constitution in May 2018. The Amendment had equally been introduced by referendum in 1983, when a majority of the Irish people voted to introduce a constitutional ban on termination of pregnancies as Article 40.3.3. By reason of its sensitive subject area, namely the provision of information about abortion services outside the Irish jurisdiction, the Regulation of Information Bill was referred to the Supreme Court by President Mary Robinson in March 1995, and the SCI delivered its judgment on 12 May.

As in other Article 26 judgments, this one opens with a list of key terms related to the subject areas covered by the Bill and the sections of the Constitution against which the Bill's provisions will have to be tested, as can be seen from example (1) below. What follows is a short summary of the main aspects inherent in the Bill. On a section-by-section basis, the contents of the Bill are thus reviewed and an anticipation is provided of the SCI's composition and eventual decision (2):

(1) *Constitution–Personal rights–Right to life of unborn child–Right to life of mother–Freedom to obtain and make available information relating to services lawfully available in another state–Whether such freedom extending to information relating to identity and location and method of communication with specified clinics for termination of pregnancies–Purpose of Fourteenth Amendment to Constitution–Regulation of Information (Services outside the State for Termination of Pregnancies) Bill, 1995–Constitution of Ireland, 1937, Article 40, s. 3, sub-s. 3.*

(2) Section 1 of the Regulation of Information (Services outside the State for Termination of Pregnancies) Bill, 1995, provided that

> “termination of pregnancies” means “intentional procurement of miscarriages of women who are pregnant.” […] Section 3 of the Bill dealt with the giving of Act information to the general public (as opposed to an individual woman) by means including newspapers, books, magazines, broadcasts and public meetings, other than the means specified in section 4. […] Having been passed by both Houses of the Oireachtas, the Bill was referred to the Supreme Court by the President, pursuant to Article 26 of the Constitution. *Held* by the Supreme Court (Hamilton C.J., O’Flaherty, Egan, Blayney and Denham JJ.), in deciding that the Bill was not repugnant to the provisions of the Constitution, 1, that both the Bill and the Fourteenth Amendment were concerned with the right to obtain or make available information; they did not purport to make lawful any act directly affecting the life of the unborn which would not have been lawful prior to the passing of the Fourteenth Amendment; they did not deal with the use which might be made of the information obtained thereunder; and they did not address the circumstances in which abortion might be legal inside or outside the jurisdiction.

The third step in the structure lies in a comprehensive list of the cases mentioned in the judgment, e.g. *The Adoption (No. 2) Bill, 1987* [1989] I.R. 656; [1989] I.L.R.M. 266; *The Criminal Law Jurisdiction Bill, 1975* [1977] I.R. 129; (1976) 110 I.L.T.R. 29; *The Electoral (Amendment) Bill, 1983* [1984] I.R. 268; [1984] I.L.R.M. 539 etc. In the fourth place, a substantial and often very large part of the judgment is devoted to procedure. In detail, this means that the main parties involved in proceedings are mentioned, and the respective lines of argument are presented.

As can be appreciated from (3) below, the SCI deemed it appropriate to have the case argued as follows: on the one hand, by hearing arguments against the Bill on the grounds that it infringed the right to life of the unborn and the mother; on the other hand, by hearing arguments in favour of the Bill from the Attorney General. As shown by (4), subsequently, a verbatim transcript of the hearing is made available, featuring critical exchanges between the SCI Justices and counsel opposing the Bill as well as the Attorney General himself.

On the one hand, Peter Kelly S.C. clearly espouses the view that the Bill should be rejected in that it is in breach of natural law: briefly, as long as the Eighth Amendment is there, he suggested, the primacy of life for the unborn could be questioned by neither law nor judicial interpretation of the law, whether directly or indirectly. On the other hand, the Attorney General predictably fights the Government’s corner: in this capacity, therefore, he seeks to distinguish constitutional imperatives, among which the protection of the unborn's life, from women's entitlement to receive true and accurate information about abortion services, as long as these pertain to other jurisdictions:

(3) On the 4th, 5th, 6th and 7th April, 1995, the Supreme Court (Hamilton C.J., O'Flaherty, Egan, Blayney and Denham JJ.) heard argument from counsel assigned by the Court to oppose the Bill on the basis of the right to life of the unborn, counsel assigned to oppose the Bill on the basis of the right to life of the mother; and from the Attorney General.

(4) *Hamilton C.J*: Is not the role of this Court, on a reference pursuant to Article 26, expressly confined to a consideration of whether the Bill, or any part of it, is repugnant to any of the provisions of the Constitution?

Peter Kelly S.C.: The point is that natural law is the ultimate governor of all the laws of men [...]. For as long as the present constitution remains in force, nothing in it or in any laws passed by the Oireachtas, or any interpretation thereof by the judiciary can run counter to the natural law. The natural law is clear–nobody may directly or intentionally take human life either born or unborn.

Hamilton C.J: Is not that view inconsistent with *The Attorney General v. X*? Did not that case examine the whole issue very carefully and conclude that in certain circumstances the right to life of the mother may prevail over the right to life of the unborn?

Peter Kelly S.C: That case is of very little binding authority. [...]

Blayney J: What do you say to Mr. Kelly's submission that the provision of names and addresses constitutes promotion?

The Attorney General: The provision of factual information is permitted by the Fourteenth Amendment and does not constitute promotion; what the Bill does is to say that the provision of factual information must not be accompanied by advocacy or promotion.

Hamilton C.J: But even if one assumes that the information is factual, is not the very act of providing it assisting in the destruction of the life of the unborn? Is it not the first step?

The Attorney General: If one looks for the "first step" that must surely be the very fact of informing someone about abortion. It must be remembered that we are talking about a constitutional entitlement to give or receive this information. The Bill is about regulating this

> entitlement; the Bill cannot take the entitlement way. The entitlement is not confined to women in the "X category".

The last part of the judgment is by all means the most important and interesting from the point of view of argumentation analysis. It contains the SCI's decision in its most elaborate form. While the substance of the Court's views on the constitutionality of the Bill has been included at an earlier stage, the Court's argumentation is now presented in full here. As required by Article 26.2.2 (cf. example 16 in Chapter 4), the Court delivers its judgment as a single entity and its reasoned decision is announced and justified by the Chief Justice. Typically, s/he begins by going back to the terms of the reference, namely when the Bill was referred to the SCI, its long title and a summary of its main provisions.

Moreover, whether as part of the running text or within a dedicated section, the Chief Justice articulates an important principle behind the Court's jurisprudence on Article 26, that is the presumption of constitutionality of the Bill. On the basis of previous judgments recalled in the text, the point is made that the Court's reasoning unfolds by considering that "the Bill having been passed by both Houses of the Oireachtas, is entitled to the presumption that no provision thereof is repugnant to the Constitution". In brief, the expectation is always that the whole of proceedings, procedures, discretions and adjudications permitted or prescribed by the Bill are intended to be conducted pursuant to the principles of constitutional justice. In addition, it is presumed that having to choose between two or more constructions of the terms of the Bill, the one that is in accordance with the provisions of the Constitution is to prevail over any other. This implies that the SCI carries an onerous burden of proof in arguing that the Bill is incompatible with *Bunreacht na hÉireann* in whole or in part.

In what follows, the Chief Justice mentions the constitutional provisions particularly involved by the reference and s/he quotes relevant passages from Articles of and successive Amendments to the constitutional text. This is of vital importance because the core of the SCI's argumentative discourse will then be revolving around the letter and/or the spirit of such provisions, an excerpt from which is provided in (5) for the case now under investigation. The rest of the decision is the actual backbone of the Court's reasoning: as such, it displays pragmatic argumentation though one of its variants and will be examined in more detail in Section 6.3:

(5) Article 40, s. 3 of the Constitution provides that:
1. The State guarantees in its laws to respect, and, as far as practicable, by its laws to defend and vindicate the personal rights of the citizen.
2. The State shall, in particular, by its laws protect as best it may from unjust attack and, in the case of injustice done, vindicate the life, person, good name, and property rights of every citizen.
3. The State acknowledges the right to life of the unborn and, with due regard to the equal right to life of the mother, guarantees in its laws to respect, and as far as practicable, by its laws to defend and vindicate that right [Hereinafter referred to as the Eighth Amendment]. This sub-section shall not limit freedom to travel between the State and another State [hereinafter referred to as the Thirteenth Amendment]. This sub-section shall not limit freedom to obtain or make available, in the State, subject to such conditions as may be laid down by law, information relating to services lawfully available in another State [hereinafter referred to as the Fourteenth Amendment].

6.3 Pragmatic argumentation in the SCI's discourse

The relevance of pragmatic argumentation as a sub-type of causal argumentation to judicial reasoning has been underlined in a wide range of publications, as we saw in Chapter 2. As far as the *SCI_26* corpus is concerned, there is clear evidence of the relationship between the Court's decisions and specific variants of the argument scheme, as illustrated in the two subsections that follow. The first (6.3.1) is devoted to the SCI's decisions in favour of the constitutionality of bills, while the second (6.3.2) is about those dismissing proposed legislation as repugnant to *Bunreacht na hÉireann*.

6.3.1 Pragmatic argumentation in favour of constitutionality

First of all, there seems a close correlation between SCI decisions to uphold the constitutionality of bills and the deployment of Variant III of pragmatic argumentation. Following Van Poppel (2012, 100), this variant can be schematised as follows:

(6) 1. Action X should be performed
1.1a Action X does not lead to Y
1.1b Y is undesirable
1.1a-1.1b' (If Action X does not lead to Y and Y is undesirable, then Action X should be performed)

This variant also applies to the Article 26 reference we chose as an example in the prior section. Here, as well as elsewhere, *Action X* lies in the SCI's interpretation of the Bill as being in accordance with the Constitution. Needless to say, *Y* as well as the nature of its undesirability change from one reference to another and will be explored in this section both in the matter of the Regulation of Information Bill, 1995 and in relation to The Emergency Powers Bill, 1976. In the former case we are now analysing, the SCI begins by laying emphasis on the consistency of the Bill with the letter of both the Thirteenth and the Fourteenth Amendment (cf. example 5 above). Since the Bill is ultimately concerned with the regulation of the process by which Irish women may access termination services abroad, nothing in the Bill exceeds the limits set by the Thirteenth Amendment ("…shall not limit freedom to travel between the State and another State…"). Furthermore, Hamilton C.J. draws the attention to the Fourteenth Amendment, which lays down that no constitutional provision shall "limit freedom to obtain or make available, in the State, subject to such conditions **as may be laid down by law**, information relating to services lawfully available in another State". As he points out, great significance should be attached to the appended clause in bold typeface, as can be seen from the short passage in (7):

(7) The provisions of the Fourteenth Amendment give to the Oireachtas, which by virtue of the provisions of Article 15, s. 2, sub-s. 1 of the Constitution has vested in it the sole and exclusive power of making laws for the State, *the power to lay down by law the conditions* to which the obtaining or making available within the State of information relating to services lawfully available in another State may be subject. […] In passing the Bill, the Oireachtas was essentially engaged *in laying down the conditions* subject to which such information should be obtained or made available and in doing so was engaged in the balancing of constitutional rights and duties, including the right to life of the unborn, the right to life of the mother, the right to information and other constitutional rights.

Hamilton C.J.'s view will not come as a surprise to the attentive reader. In fact, *as may be laid down by law* can be associated with the empowering function we attributed to other clauses of the same kind in Chapter 4 (e.g., examples 1, 4 and 5 of Section 4.3). Within the clause itself is squeezed the *Oireachtas*' right to set out the *conditions* under which women are free to obtain information relating to abortion services lawfully available in another State. It is indeed interesting that what was quintessentially linguistic observation based on corpus analysis on our part, basically informs the Chief Justice's reasoning at the outset.

It follows from this preliminary reading of the Bill that its terms are broadly acceptable in light of the general framework provided by the Constitution. What needs to be assessed by the Court is therefore whether the provisions of the Bill represent a fair and reasonable balancing by the *Oireachtas* of the various conflicting rights and are not so contrary to reason and fairness as to constitute an unjust attack on the constitutional rights of the unborn or on the constitutional rights of the mother or any other person or persons. In other words, the compatibility of the Bill ought to be considered with the rights of the two main legal subjects embedded in Article 40.3.3 as a result of the Eighth Amendment, namely the unborn and the mother.

As far as the unborn is concerned, Hamilton C.J. focuses on the mechanisms provided by the Bill to give women information about abortion services abroad. First of all, he notes, the Bill is fairly restrictive in terms of the channels through which such information is imparted: accordingly, displaying notices or advertisements in public places or distributing books, newspapers, journals, magazines, leaflets or pamphlets do not constitute accepted practices advocated by the Bill. Quite the opposite (example 8 below), the requirement that information be truthful and objective and *does not advocate or promote* terminations of pregnancies ensures that the rights of the unborn are neither curtailed nor infringed.

As regards the mother's rights, the fact that abortion services may in no way be promoted guarantees that doctors are in a favourable position to relay full information regarding the woman's state of health, the effects pregnancy might have on it, and the *consequences to her health and life* in case the pregnancy continues. The mother's rights are therefore unaffected (9), because in no way do the provisions in the Bill prevent her from making *an informed decision* about the termination of her pregnancy (abroad) or its continuation (wherever she chooses).

(8) The giving of information to the public is further restricted by the provisions of s. 4 of the Bill which provides that it shall not be lawful to display a notice (including an advertisement) containing information, to which the Bill applies, in or at a place to which the public have access whether upon payment or free of charge or to distribute without solicitation by the recipients a book, newspaper, journal, magazine, leaflet or pamphlet, or any other document, or a film or a recording (whether of sound or images or both) containing such information. The requirement that the information to be given relates only to services lawfully available outside the State, is truthful and objective, and does not advocate or promote and is not accompanied by any advocacy or promotion of the termination of pregnancy

represents a fair and reasonable balancing by the Oireachtas of the conflicting rights herein and is not so contrary to reason and fairness as to constitute an unjust attack on the constitutional rights of the unborn or any other person.

(9) While a doctor is precluded by the terms of the Bill from advocating or promoting the termination of pregnancy, he is not in any way precluded from giving full information to a woman with regard to her state of health, the effect of the pregnancy thereon and the consequences to her health and life if the pregnancy continues and leaving to the mother the decision whether in all the circumstances the pregnancy should be terminated. The doctor is not in any way prohibited from giving to his pregnant patient all the information necessary to enable her to make an informed decision provided that he does not advocate or promote the termination of pregnancy.

These extracts form an integral part of Hamilton C.J.'s pragmatic argumentation. Going back to Variant III as schematised in (6) above, the Court's interpretation of the Bill (*Action X*), notably that it "is not repugnant to the Constitution or to any provision thereof" must be read in relation to what the SCI sees as undesirable. In the present case, *Y* is any unjust attack on the constitutional rights of the unborn along with the mother. By reading through (8) and (9) taken together, therefore, the decision to uphold the constitutionality of the Bill is justified on the grounds that none of its provisions produce the undesirable outcome of violating the rights of the two subjects safeguarded by the Constitution and its successive amendments.

In discussing the implementation of the subordinate argumentation on which pragmatic argumentation rests, Feteris (2016, 67) suggests that this forms a reaction to the critical question "Is the result [Y] really (un)desirable from a legal point of view?". In response to the critical question as applied to the judgment we have been examining so far, it can be said that the undesirability of *Y* from a legal point of view stems from its inherent incompatibility with a purpose or goal P intended by the Constitution's drafters. In this case, purpose or goal P is the acknowledgment and protection of the rights of both unborn and mother (as of Article 40.3.3), coalescing as they should be with the freedom to travel and obtain information relating to abortion services overseas (as of the Thirteenth and Fourteenth Amendment). In the SCI's decision as announced by Hamilton C.J., the Regulation of Information (Services outside the State for Termination of Pregnancies) Bill, 1995 leaves the attainment of P unprejudiced and as such is not repugnant to the Constitution.

The correlation between Variant III in the Court's pragmatic argumentation and decisions to affirm the constitutionality of Bills is demonstrated by the other judgments in the corpus. Among these, that we will most extensively deal with relates to The Emergency Powers Bill, 1976 [1977, 1 I.R]. On 1 September 1976, *Dáil Éireann* adopted the following resolution: "That [...], arising out of the armed conflict now taking place in Northern Ireland, a national emergency exists affecting the vital interests of the State." On the same day, *Seanad Éireann* passed a resolution along the same lines. This formed the core of a Bill whose long title was as follows: "An Act for the purpose of securing the public safety and the preservation of the State in time of an armed conflict in respect of which each of the Houses of the Oireachtas has adopted a resolution on the first day of September, 1976, pursuant to subsection 3 of section 3 of Article 28 of the Constitution."

The relevant Article of the *Bunreacht* refers to laws the *Oireachtas* is entitled to enact "for the purpose of securing the public safety and the preservation of the State in time of war or armed rebellion" (Article 28.3.3). In particular, the phrase *time of war* is taken to denote armed conflicts in which the State is not directly involved but from which a national emergency is established to have arisen in a way that jeopardises the vital interests of the State. Briefly, the Constitution entertains the notion of special legislation to be enacted to respond to an emergency and remain in force until after the war, armed conflict or armed rebellion, when both Houses of the *Oireachtas* have resolved that the emergency has ceased to exist.

The nature of the Emergency Powers Bill was controversial for two main reasons. The first was the presence of radical measures such as Section 2, which provided that a member of *An Garda Síochána*[1] may "without warrant stop, search, question and arrest any person, or do any one or more of those things in respect of any person, if he suspects with reasonable cause that that person has committed, is committing or is about to commit an offence under the Offences against the State Act, 1939" or other scheduled offences, or if they suspect with reasonable cause that "that person is carrying any document or other article or thing, or is in possession of information, relating to the commission or intended commission of the offence".

The second reason lay in the implementation of norms giving such considerable discretion to police authorities in the light of the opening

[1] This the Republic of Ireland's national police and security service (see https://www.garda.ie/en/. Accessed May 22, 2020).

lines of Article 28.3.3. The Article lays down that "nothing" in the Constitution "shall be invoked to invalidate any law enacted by the Oireachtas for the purpose of securing public safety and the preservation of the State" in time of emergency, nor "nullify any act done or purporting to be done in time of war or armed rebellion in pursuance of any such law". In other words, there was fear that the free exercise of the powers justified in the Bill could in no way be limited by constitutional guarantees. After the Emergency Powers Bill was passed by both Houses of the *Oireachtas*, therefore, President Cearbhall Ó Dálaigh decided to refer it to the Supreme Court under Article 26.

In the SCI's judgment delivered by O'Higgins C.J., the constitutionality of the Bill is assessed in the light of a comprehensive reading of the Constitution as a whole. Having heard arguments by the Attorney General and his counsel as well as by counsel assigned by the Court, what was canvassed in argument was precisely the extent to which the Bill, if signed by the President and lent constitutional validity under Article 28.3.3, would encroach on personal rights that would otherwise enjoy full constitutional protection. The crucial passage in the Court's reasoning is reported in example (10):

> (10) In this context it is important to point out that when a law is saved from invalidity by Article 28, s. 3, sub-s. 3, the prohibition against invoking the Constitution in reference to it is only if the invocation is for the purpose of invalidating it. *For every other purpose the Constitution may be invoked.* Thus, a person detained under s. 2 of the bill may not only question the legality of his detention if there has been non-compliance with the express requirements of s. 2, but may also rely on provisions of the Constitution for the purpose of construing that section and of testing the legality of what has been done in purported operation of it. […] While it is not necessary to embark upon an exploration of all the incidents or characteristics which may not accompany the arrest and custody of a person under that section, it is nevertheless desirable, in view of the submissions made to the Court, to state that the section *is not to be read as an abnegation of the arrested person's rights* (constitutional or otherwise) in respect of matters such as the right of communication, the right to have legal and medical assistance, and the right of access to the Courts. If the section were used in breach of such rights the High Court might grant an order for release under the provisions for habeas corpus contained in the Constitution.

As was the case with the Regulation of Information Bill, here as well does the SCI seem to set its decision against the background of the undesirability of a result to be avoided. By applying the schematisation in (6) to the present judgment, *Y* is the *abnegation* of an arrested person's rights *in respect of matters such as the right of communication, the right to have legal and medical assistance, and the right of access to the Courts*. The prohibition against invoking the Constitution in relation to emergency legislation under Article 28.3.3, so the argument goes, only stands in case the invocation is intended to invalidate the law. Against this backdrop, since the SCI's eventual decision that the Emergency Powers Bill was not repugnant to the Constitution (*Action X*) left all constitutional safeguards for *habeas corpus* rights unprejudiced, it was the right decision in the Court's opinion. In response to the critical question "Is the result [Y] really (un)desirable from a legal point of view?", there is indeed no doubt as to the undesirability of *Y* from a legal point of view in regard to its incompatibility with goal P intended by the Constitution's drafters as the enforcement of fundamental rights such as *habeas corpus* guarantees.

Even without going into as much detail as for the two judgments discussed so far, it is interesting that Variant III as the preferred configuration, as it were, of the Court's reasoning underlying decisions in favour of the constitutionality of bills is confirmed in the other Article 26 references in the corpus. Thus, for instance, it is equally valuable evidence that the Variant may be observed to be at work in a judgment that outdates that for the Emergency Powers Bill 1976 by far yet addresses similar matters. In relation to the Offences against the State (Amendment) Bill 1940, the piece of legislation in question contained measures that also seemed to affect *habeas corpus* rights.

In Section 4 of the Bill, the principle is outlined that a Minister of State is entitled to order the arrest of any person he believes to be engaged in activities prejudicial to the preservation of public peace, order or the security of the State "by warrant under his hand and sealed with his official seal". The Constitution admittedly considers the case of minor offences to be tried by courts of summary jurisdiction as well as the establishment of "special courts" as required by the "preservation of public peace and order" (Art. 38.2-3). Nonetheless, the SCI argued that that did not *take away the right to habeas corpus*. In so far as the substance of Article 40.4.2 is reaffirmed (example 11), the proposed bill would not produce such undesirable result (*Y*). No matter the extent to which the Bill *will have the effect of altering the law*, therefore, the High Court may still order that the body of a detained person be produced as well as the "release of such person" from detention "unless satisfied that he is being detained in accordance with the law" (Article 40.4.2):

(11) It was contended that the effect of the Bill is to take away the right to *habeas corpus*. There is no foundation for this contention. Notwithstanding the provisions of the Bill, a person who is detained is entitled under Article 40, clause 4, par. 2, to have the legality of his detention enquired into and to obtain an order for his release, unless the Court or Judge, enquiring into the matter, is satisfied that all the provisions of the Bill have been complied with and that the detention is legal. No doubt the Bill, when enacted, will have the effect of altering the law and, to that extent, will justify a detention which might otherwise be unlawful. This, however, cannot rightly be described as taking away the right to *habeas corpus*.

In the case of the Electoral (Amendment) Bill 1961, in addition, Variant III again permeates the whole of the SCI's argumentation in spite of the somewhat less pressing matter approached by the Bill. This had been conceived as an act to set the number of TDs, revise their constituencies and amend the law regarding their election. In assessing the constitutionality of the Bill, the Supreme Court referred to the letter of Article 16.2.3, which provides that "the ratio between the number of members to be elected at any time for each constituency and the population of each constituency, as ascertained at the last preceding census, shall, **so far as it is practicable**, be the same throughout the country". In response to objections raised against the Bill as exceeding the ratio to be determined in accordance with the Constitution, the SCI ruled that the *divergence* caused by the Bill in terms of the ratio was *within reasonable limits* and as such fell within the practicability scope defined by the above Article. The danger of disrupting the balance sought by the *Bunreacht* having been averted (*Y*), the Bill was found not to be repugnant to the Constitution (12):

(12) To justify the Court in holding that the sub-section has been infringed it must, however, be shown that the failure to maintain the ratio between the number of members for each constituency and the population of each constituency involves such a divergence as to make it clear that the Oireachtas has not carried out the intention of the sub-clause. In the opinion of the Court *the divergencies shown in the Bill are within reasonable limits*. Accordingly, the Court is of opinion that this ground of objection has not been established.

6.3.2 Pragmatic argumentation against constitutionality

SCI decisions to declare bills unconstitutional are not as univocally associated with one specific variant of pragmatic argumentation. However, evidence suggests that the Court's interpretation of bills as repugnant mainly involves the use of Variant IV, which can be schematised as in (13) below, again following Van Poppel (2012, 101):

(13) 1. Action X should not be performed
1.1a Action X does not lead to Y
1.1b Y is desirable
1.1a-1.1b' (If Action X does not lead to Y and Y is desirable, then Action X should not be performed)

The presence of the variant was established through judgments such as that related to the Health (Amendment) (No. 2) Bill, 2004 and the Matrimonial Home Bill, 1993. The Health Bill had been introduced to amend a section of the Health Act, 1970. The subject matter of the Bill was confined to the payment of certain charges by certain categories of persons, in most cases elderly persons of limited means. These would benefit in the future or had benefited in the past from being maintained in a hospital or home by a health board. In the former instance, the relevant provisions of the Bill were to operate prospectively, and in the latter retrospectively. For the purposes of its consideration of whether any provision of the Bill was repugnant to the Constitution, the Court was satisfied that the correct approach was to interpret the Bill in the light of Articles 43 and 40.3.2.

While Article 43 defends property rights, Article 40.3.2 imposes on the State the duty to "protect as best it may from unjust attack and, in the case of injustice done, vindicate the life, good name, and property rights of every citizen". As a result, the SCI proceeded by, first of all, examining the nature of the property rights at issue; secondly, by considering whether the Bill consisted of a regulation of those rights in accordance with principles of social justice and whether the Bill was required so as to delimit those rights in accordance with the exigencies of the common good; thirdly, on the grounds of its conclusions on these issues, by considering whether the Bill constituted an unjust attack on those property rights.

In this case, therefore, *Y* (as in 13 above) was the preservation of citizens' right to the private ownership of external goods. The desirability of *Y* from a legal point of view was evaluated by the Court in terms of the compatibility with goal P. This was intended by the Constitution's drafters as the protection of personal rights with particular reference to the case of people from the more vulnerable sections of society and potentially more readily exposed to the risk of unjust attack. As can be seen from (14), the Court pronounced against the Bill's constitutionality with regard to the retrospective provisions of the Bill itself. These were identified as abrogating the right of persons otherwise entitled to do so *to recover monies for charges unlawfully imposed upon them in the past for the provision of certain in-patient services*. By way of a broad interpretation of Article 43, the Court considered that the constitutional safeguard of property rights may not be construed as encompassing *only property rights which are of great value*. It follows that the limit imposed by the Bill on the right of certain people to recover sums they had unjustly paid was read by the SCI as an infringement of their property rights and a kind of unjust attack on them by the State. Briefly, since the Bill failed to vindicate these people's property rights, it was to be proclaimed as repugnant to the Constitution:

> (14) The retrospective provisions of the Bill are those which abrogate the right of persons, otherwise entitled to do so, to recover monies for charges unlawfully imposed upon them in the past for the provision of certain in-patient services. […] The court considers that the right to recover monies for the charges thus imposed is a property right of the persons concerned which is protected by Articles 43 and 40.3.2 of the Constitution from, *inter alia*, unjust attack by the State. The Constitution, in protecting property rights, does not encompass only property rights which are of great value. It protects such rights even when they are of modest value and in particular, as in this case, where the persons affected are among the more vulnerable sections of society and might more readily be exposed to the risk of unjust attack. For the reasons expressed in this judgment, the court has decided that the retrospective provisions of the Bill contained in s. 1(b) which provide for the insertion of subss. (5), (6) and (7), and subsection (11), insofar as it defines "relevant charge", in s. 53 of the Act of 1970, are repugnant to the Constitution and in particular Articles 43 and 40.3.2 thereof.

As we said earlier on, Variant IV also applies to the Matrimonial Home Bill, 1993. The Bill had been introduced to make provision in the interest of the common good in relation to the ownership of matrimonial homes, to provide for certain other matters affecting spouses in relation to property and to provide for related matters. Thus, for instance, the Bill stated that, in the case of dwellings occupied by a married couple in which either or both spouses had or had had an interest but which was not owned by them as joint tenants or as tenants in common in equal shares, the interest in the dwelling would vest in both spouses as joint tenants.

In reviewing the Bill, the SCI regarded the defence of the family's "authority" (Article 41.2) as the legally desirable aim *Y* instrumental in realising goal P intended by the Constitution's drafters as the recognition of "the Family as the natural primary and fundamental unit group of Society" (Article 41.1). On the one hand, the SCI accepted that the provisions of this Bill were directed to encourage the joint ownership of matrimonial homes and that such an objective was clearly an important element of the common good conducive to the stability of marriage and the general protection of the institution of the family. On the other hand, however, the Bill was interpreted by the Court as representing a disproportionate intervention by the State with family rights as inalienable, imprescriptible, *antecedent and superior to all positive law*. At its simplest, the Court's line of argument was that by superimposing the Bill's framework on families' own *right to make decisions*, its provisions failed to achieve the desirable aim *to protect the authority of the family* (*Y*) and as such were to be dismissed as repugnant to the Constitution (15):

(15) Having regard to the extreme importance of the authority of the family as acknowledged in Article 41 of the Constitution and to the acceptance in that Article of the fact that the rights which attach to the family including its right to make decisions within its authority are inalienable and imprescriptible and antecedent and superior to all positive law, the Court is satisfied that such provisions do not constitute reasonably proportionate intervention by the State with the rights of the family and constitute a failure by the State to protect the authority of the family.

Although Variant IV has the lion's share in decisions to declare bills repugnant to the Constitution, Variant II is also occasionally represented. Van Poppel (2012, 99-100) schematises this variant as in (16) below:

(16) 1. Action X should not be performed
1.1a Action X leads to Y
1.1b Y is undesirable
1.1a-1.1b' (If Action X leads to Y and Y is undesirable, then Action X should not be performed)

The Article 26 reference related to the School Attendance Bill 1942 may be taken as an instance of Variant II at work. The Bill had been designed by the *Oireachtas* to make further and better provisions to ensure school attendance by children to whom its predecessor, namely the School Attendance Act 1926, applied. At the outset, the Bill was rather strict in that it required parents to have children attend "a national school, a suitable school, or a recognised school, on every day on which such school is open for secular instruction and for such time on such day as shall be prescribed or sanctioned by the Minister in respect of such day". Among the most heftily disputed norms, more specifically, was subsection 1 of section 4, which prescribed that children would not be deemed to be receiving suitable education in a manner other than by attending school, unless such education and the manner in which children received it had been certified by the Minister to be suitable.

The yardstick by which to measure the Bill's constitutionality turned out to be Section 3 of Article 42 of *Bunreacht na hÉireann*. In paragraph 1, to begin with, the State is prohibited–*the State shall not* in English; *ní cead don Stát* [it is not permitted to the State] in Irish–from obliging parents "in violation of their conscience to send children to schools established by the State, or to any particular type of school designated by the State". Moreover, paragraph 2 provides as follows: "The State shall, however, as guardian of the common good, require in view of actual conditions that the children receive **a certain minimum education**, moral, intellectual and social". The phrasing of the paragraph suggests a link between the common good to be envisaged by the State and a minimum standard of education for children.

In these respects, the wording of subsection 1 of the Bill's fourth section put the Minister for Education in a rather invidious position, the SCI found. By laying down that both the education itself and the manner in which children would be receiving it were to be certified by the Minister, the Bill appeared to exceed the limits permitted by the Constitution and was therefore rejected as repugnant to it. As is shown by (17) below, the problem with the proposed legislation seems to have been that its adoption would have produced the undesirable outcome *Y* (cf. 16) of allowing the State to interfere with the "certain minimum of education" to be received by children and the manner to give as well as receive it. The undesirability of *Y* from a legal point of view lies in its inherent incompatibility with goal P intended by the Constitution's drafters as the parents' right to supply the general standard of education set by the *Bunreacht* as a "minimum":

(17) We are of opinion that the section is open to objection from a constitutional point of view [...]. Under sub-s. 1 not only the education, but also the manner in which such child is receiving it must be certified by the Minister. We do not consider that this is warranted by the Constitution. The State is entitled to require that children shall receive a certain minimum education. So long as parents supply this general standard of education we are of opinion that the manner in which it is being given and received is entirely a matter for the parents and is not a matter in respect of which the State under the Constitution is entitled to interfere.

6.4 Conclusions

In this chapter, evidence has been provided about two key aspects of relevance to this research. Not surprisingly, the first is that the Constitution's centrality to the Irish public sphere is apparent from Article 26 judgments, as far as specialised discourse is concerned. The second is the important role of pragmatic argumentation in the Supreme Court's reasoning. Unlike in legal theory including research on the Irish legal system (see Chapter 1), the emphasis here was more on argumentation than procedure *per se*.

In her study on prototypical argumentative patterns in a legal context, Feteris (2016) shows that pragmatic argumentation in legal justification can be reconstructed in terms of judges' dialectical obligations. These define the dialectically relevant moves in the justification of legal decisions in that they prescribe the elements of the justification required from the perspective of the dialectical role of judges to account for the different decisions and choices in the discussion process. She therefore translates the arguments put forward as reactions to various forms of critique that are legally relevant in terms of parts of a prototypical argumentative pattern.

The analysis in the chapter expands on Feteris's contribution in two main respects. First of all, while her theorisation on pragmatic argumentation ultimately focuses on a single text, the present study draws on a larger data set through the 15 judgments in the *SCI_26* corpus. Secondly, it combines her insights on pragmatic argumentation in a legal context with the identification of specific variants of the scheme based on Van Poppel's (2012) categorisation. The integration of such perspectives enabled us to systematically associate the deployment of pragmatic argumentation with the SCI's rulings in favour or against the constitutionality of the bills referred to it by successive Irish Presidents. This led us to shed light on the way the letter as well as the spirit of *Bunreacht na hÉireann* provisions of various sorts inform the views of SCI Justices as guardians of constitutional rights and guarantees.

Furthermore, the articulation of Variants III, IV and II in the Court's discourse as documented in Subsections 6.3.1 and 6.3.2 shows added analytical value, because the judgements discussed in more detail here found an echo not simply in the courtroom, but in Irish society at large. Accordingly, the SCI's decision to pronounce in favour of the Regulation of Information (Services outside the State for Termination of Pregnancies) Bill 1995 underpinned the decision of many an Irish woman to collect information about abortion clinics abroad, thereby bringing an already existing yet arguably underestimated issue into public spotlight. In fact, based on statistics from the UK Department of Health reported by *The Irish Times*, a total of 168,705 Irish women travelled from the Republic into Britain alone between 1980 and 2016.[2] The decision to legitimise the presence of abortion in public discourse, however still in the presence of the Eighth Amendment in the Constitution, might be said to have served as a gradual build-up to the campaign that would eventually lead to the repeal of the Eighth in May 2018.

Likewise, the ruling in favour of the constitutionality of the Emergency Powers Bill 1976 was not devoid of political implications. The passing of the Bill itself had ignited fierce controversy. What seemed almost inevitable at the outset was actually that such an Act could set at nothing other rights guaranteed elsewhere in the Constitution. In order to pass any legislation, many protested, governments with effective majority support only needed to get both Houses of the *Oireachtas* to pass a resolution that an emergency existed and then push through legislation in the name of the preservation of public safety. At its most extreme, the objection was voiced, legislation proscribing opposition parties, outlawing elections or imposing draconian measures in response to minor transgressions of the law would escape the courts' scrutiny. As Gallagher (2005, 79-80) rightly points out, the Supreme Court's judgment pronounced the Bill non-repugnant to the Constitution yet tempered the potential side effects of Article 28.3.3:

> While not disputing the right of the Oireachtas to enact any legislation it saw fit in order to preserve public safety and the state once an emergency had been declared, the Court said that it 'expressly reserves for future consideration' the question of whether it had the right to consider whether the Oireachtas was justified in declaring that a national emergency existed. No case has arisen subsequently to test the way in which the courts' thinking on this issue has developed, but the warning shot sounded in 1976 may have counterbalanced to some extent the action of the Oireachtas in 1939 and 1941 in widening the scope of Article 28.3.3.

Even so, the hostility aroused by the Bill or at least the decision to refer it to the Supreme Court under Article 26 was not to cease forthwith. Soon after the Court's judgment, Minister for Defence Patrick Donegan

---

[2] *The Irish Times*. 2018. "Fact check–Have more than 170,000 Irish women travelled abroad for an abortion?". Accessed February 7, 2020. https://www.irishtimes.com/news/politics/fact-check-have-more-than-170-000-irish-women-travelled-abroad-for-an-abortion-1.3481581.

reportedly referred to President Ó Dálaigh as "a thundering disgrace" for submitting the Bill to the SCI at all. The then *Taoiseach* Liam Cosgrave refused to dismiss the Minister for his comment, while Donegan himself survived a motion of no confidence in the *Dáil*. As a result of the outcome of the vote, the President handed in his resignation (Elgie and Fitzgerald 2015).

The findings from this chapter demonstrate how the reasoning behind such momentous decisions took shape, and they show what rhetorical tools are developed by SCI Justices as they decide what the Constitution is, so to speak. This chapter concludes the analytical part of the volume. To begin with, Chapter 4 focused on the peculiarities of the Irish Constitution we studied as a corpus from a linguistic point of view. Then, the research examined the role of *Bunreacht na hÉireann* in the Irish public sphere. In the first place (Chapter 5), the reaction to the Constitution's enactment in 1937 was gauged by looking at the lexical and argumentative strategies through which two prominent national newspapers (*Irish Independent* and *Irish Press*) represented and in many respects constructed the Constitution of Ireland for the respective readership. Finally (Chapter 6), the analysis of the Supreme Court's argumentation in Article 26 judgments provided evidence about how the *Bunreacht* has come to life in judicial discourse revolving around the charter's provisions. In the next chapter, the findings will be briefly discussed in relation to the research questions outlined in Chapter 1, and the paths of further research the book may open up.

CHAPTER SEVEN

DISCUSSION AND CONCLUSIONS

7.1 Introduction

In Chapters 4-6, the findings of our study of the language of the Irish Constitution and its role in Irish public life were reported. It is the purpose of this chapter to conclude the volume by discussing these findings in two main ways. First of all, the answer to the research questions in Section 1.1 is provided (Section 7.2). Secondly, suggestions are put forward about paths of further research the book may have carved out (7.3).

7.2 Wrapping up: An answer to the research questions

The specific data from each of the three strands in the investigation have been discussed at the end of the respective chapters. In this section, to begin with, a more general answer is provided to the leading questions posed at the outset of the research.

(1) Why has the Constitution been such a key document for the Republic?

The answer to this question has been provided in Chapter 1. The overview of scholarly literature offered there allowed us to set the *Bunreacht* against its own historical background and examine a number of distinctive aspects of the document. In particular, the coverage of the contentious provisions on sovereignty and fundamental (as well as unenumerated) rights shed light on the Constitution as a thoroughly debated charter over the years in which it has been in force. Moreover, controversy over canons of constitutional interpretation, the conceptualisation of women, the influence of Roman Catholicism and even language issues arising from the bilingual version of the text provide evidence that the *Bunreacht* has marked the stages through which the country has developed since Independence. This means that, as with all fundamental laws, the Irish Constitution was meant to stay and regulate politics and society well beyond the decade when it was drafted. However, the document has had to be amended or at least reinterpreted by taking stock of the dramatic changes undergone by the Republic over the last forty years.

Accordingly, Irish women can be acknowledged to have played a vital part in Irish society. To give but one example, it was under the presidency of Mary Robinson (1990-1997) and Mary McAleese (1997-2011) that important and powerful gestures were made about the need for a more mature and inclusive concept of Irish identity. This was symbolized by Remembrance Day, when all Irish men and women who died as a result of war are commemorated, a moment signifying a growing maturity within Irish nationalism under the aegis of the first female Irish Presidents (Ferriter 2005). While this has been the case, the fact remains that the Constitution still contains norms that envisage women's role in Irish society in somewhat restrictive terms.

In addition, whereas the *Bunreacht* still displays signs of the Catholic Church's influence, as in the Preamble, it was interesting to see that provisions such as that recognising the special position of the Church or the Eighth Amendment itself have now been dropped. This seems to stimulate widespread public discussion about how Catholic doctrine may have to revisit or reconsider its position in Irish society. Moreover, the introduction of successive amendments to the Constitution has posed the problem of consistency from a linguistic point view, as far as the Irish-language version of it is concerned. Finally, it is ever fascinating to see how constitutional interpretation has tried to hold on to the values still acting as the cornerstones for the Irish polity, and at the same time accommodate the demands for change from a more open and secular citizenship.

The challenges posed to the solidity of the Constitution as a pillar of social order, but also its historical significance in the light of Ireland's rich cultural heritage, and even the way language is used to convey key meanings across sections of the charter (Chapter 4) equally contribute to rendering this text well worth examining at the present time.

(2) What was (/is) the impact of the Constitution on Irish public discourse at both a popular and a specialised level?

A joint reading of Chapters 1 and 4 is supposed to have satisfied the curiosity of readers interested in the distinctive institutional implications behind and discourse features of *Bunreacht na hÉireann*. The following chapters then shifted our perspective to the public reception and institutional application, as it were, of Ireland's charter. In order to evaluate its impact on Irish public discourse, two case studies were undertaken, the first on the Irish press as an example of popular discourse, the second on Supreme Court judgments as representative of specialised discourse. The findings from these studies helped answer the third and fourth research questions, respectively.

(3) How was the Constitution represented and "argued" by the Irish press upon its enactment?

In order to answer this question, a corpus of news texts (*Bunreacht_News*) from two newspapers from the mainstream Irish media, the *Irish Independent* and *Irish Press*, was designed. First of all, the editorial stance of the two newspapers was reviewed, while the subsequent analysis looked at the way the contentious issue of women's rights was dealt with from the columns of both. The analysis of argumentative discourse and underlying lexical choices has highlighted the use of news discourse in order to affect and at once reflect public perception of the historic document due to come into operation in late 1937.

In the attempt to affect the average reader's perception of the document, first of all, the two newspapers take differing viewpoints in relation to the innovations brought by Ireland's new fundamental law. On the one hand, the *Independent* voices its scepticism over both the substance of the *Bunreacht*–e.g., the powers of the new President–and the method chosen to adopt it, namely a plebiscite in favour of the Constitution by a very narrow margin. On the other hand, due to its capacity as a sounding board for *Fianna Fáil*, the *Irish Press*' adherence to the constitutional project envisaged by de Valera is beyond question.

What is noteworthy, secondly, is that the *Press*' propaganda machine, as it were, appears to work through a more extensive repertoire of rhetorical devices. Not only, therefore, do editorials extol the virtues of the Constitution, but the newspaper's praise of the charter also includes a somewhat more biased coverage of Constitution Day, as many people celebrated the *Bunreacht* coming into force. In addition, strong emphasis is laid on the Catholic Church's alignment with the principles behind the Constitution in the form of both statements from members of the Hierarchy and favourable comments from Catholic periodicals at home and abroad. Finally, the *Press* corroborates its views by favourably comparing the new Constitution with the old.

From a methodological perspective, it was significant that these findings were based on a manual investigation of the corpus texts, while argumentation analysis provided the tools to identify the commitment of each newspaper to a distinctive stance, with the two outlets often responding to each other in animated critical discussion in relation to specific issues such as women's status in the Constitution. Not only, therefore, did results show how patterns of argumentation determined the overall structure of the *Independent* and the *Press*' argumentation. They also served to project a vivid picture of the role of daily news media in orchestrating public debate on the new Constitution and its far-reaching implications for citizens present and future.

(4) How has the *Bunreacht* entered the argumentation of Irish judges across the decades, as they have been required to pronounce on the compatibility of proposed legislation with its norms?

In Chapter 6, a case study was undertaken on the impact of the Republic's fundamental law on the judiciary. In particular, the Supreme Court of Ireland's argumentation was examined in the context of Article 26 references. To begin with, the prototypical structure of Article 26 judgments was reviewed, in order to get readers to familiarise themselves with their overall textual organisation. In addition, the findings from a qualitative investigation of the 15 judgments in the *SCI_26* corpus were presented. As we saw, data showed that pragmatic argumentation lies at the heart of the Supreme Court's discourse.

In the first place, a close correlation was established between SCI decisions to uphold the constitutionality of bills and the deployment of Variant III of pragmatic argumentation. In this context, the action of interpreting a bill as being in accordance with the Constitution is advocated on the grounds that it would produce no undesirable outcome. Secondly, SCI decisions to declare bills unconstitutional were not as univocally associated with one specific variant of pragmatic argumentation. However, evidence suggested that the Court's interpretation of bills as repugnant mainly involves the use of Variant IV, where a ruling in favour of the compatibility of proposed legislation is presented as a dispreferred course of action in that it would bring about undesirable effects. Alternatively, the SCI's judgments against the constitutionality of bills were observed to be supported by Variant II, where a decision to the contrary is argued to be discouraged by the fact that it would determine an adverse outcome.

The variants of pragmatic argumentation reconstructed through the analysis were schematised and illustrated by referring to well-known cases included in the corpus. Furthermore, the desirability or undesirability of the effects of a decision, based on which the SCI is documented to have pronounced for or against bills' constitutionality, is shown to have been examined by the Court in terms of the compatibility with a primary goal P intended by the Constitution's drafters to be of paramount importance. Descriptive though it was, the analysis followed Feteris's (2016) theorisation, since the articulation of pragmatic argumentation was evaluated in response to the main critical question triggering the argumentation in relation to goals and values the Court considers to be crucial in the fulfilment of its functions.

The evidence provided by the chapter is valuable, because it shows how the choice of pragmatic argumentation as the prevailing scheme shapes the Supreme Court's discourse as a means to uphold what Justices see as the dominant values of Ireland as a democratic polity. As we saw, these may include, as the case may require, the State's safeguard of family authority, private property to the benefit of vulnerable people and *habeas corpus* rights, to name but a few.

7.3 Conclusions

The research presented in the volume has taken different directions. This should make it appealing to different audiences. First of all, linguists might be interested in the data reviewed in Chapter 4. Accordingly, the classic corpus analysis of frequent lexical items has shown that collocation proves a useful tool to identify recurrent phraseology. In turn, this has led us to find out about a number of key discourse functions served by phraseological units in context. In other words, the interplay of computer-assisted, corpus-driven work with sound knowledge of the context in which the Constitution was produced provided helpful insights at more than one level. For instance, it was interesting that the perspective brought by scholarly research on the Irish-language version of the *Bunreacht* could be substantiated by the finding that the choice of modal verbs seems to be governed by collocational trends, too (Section 4.3). More generally, it was significant that linguistic observation enabled us to map the text and understand how key meanings are expressed in terms of the presentation of the prerogatives of Irish institutions and political actors such as the *Taoiseach* and the President.

Secondly, news analysts might be interested in the method behind the analysis of the Irish press in Chapter 5. While Irish journalism has been a favourite object of investigation with respect to its historical evolution across centuries as well as the selection of news contents as part of historiographical works, content analysis has broadly characterised much research in the field. From such a disciplinary angle, researchers often "break down the text to identify the major subject areas which are pursued in the news, and then examine the explanatory frameworks which underpin them" (Happer and Philo 2013, 323). No doubt, this kind of qualitative approach has the merit of carrying out detailed analyses of key explanatory themes in headlines and newspaper articles. This study also brings the advantages of qualitative analysis, but it adds to it a more detailed account of the lexical choices and argument schemes underpinning the journalists' discourse.

Thirdly, the findings from Chapter 6 may appeal to argumentation analysts. The data from the *SCI_26* corpus articulate a more comprehensive view on the use of pragmatic argumentation. Not only do they more systematically account for the choice of specific variants of the scheme in relation to the Supreme Court's decisions on matters of constitutional significance, but they shed light on the way the argumentation has adapted to the context of Irish law over the years. For this reason, the analysis may also draw the attention of jurists who would like to sharpen their knowledge of Irish jurisprudence, by looking at argument patterns at work in the SCI's discourse.

To conclude, this work may carve out paths of further research. As far as the study of argumentative discourse is concerned, for instance, two options may be considered. First of all, debate over the Constitution from the point of view of the print media could be explored through corpora including news texts published as campaigns to introduce major amendments to the *Bunreacht* were in full sway. For comparative purposes, for instance, one may focus on newspapers from 1983, when the Eighth Amendment was introduced in order to place a ban on abortion, as opposed to the same publications from 35 years later during the campaign to repeal the Eighth. In this regard, it would be fascinating to look at the changes the argumentative strategy of the same newspaper may have undergone over more than three decades of profound transformation in Irish society.

As regards judicial argumentation, secondly, the study of argument patterns in the discourse of Ireland's Supreme Court may be extended to a corpus of landmark decisions affirming unenumerated rights (cf. Section 1.3). A qualitative analysis of the judgments that revolutionised Irish constitutional history would help to show whether the identification of latent rights tended to mobilise different rhetorical resources, or at least establish peculiar patterns of coordinative or multiple argumentation. Similarly, it would be a promising direction to compare the discourse of Justices arguing in favour of the protection of unenumerated rights with that of Justices who adopted more conservative views militating against judicial activism (cf. Mac Cormaic 2016).

REFERENCES

Aarnio, Aulis. 1989. *The rational as reasonable. A treatise on legal justification*. Dordrecht: Kluwer.

Alexy, Robert. 1989 [1978]. *A theory of legal argumentation: The theory of rational discourse as theory of legal justification*. Oxford: Clarendon Press.

Anthony, Laurence. 2006. "AntConc 3.2.1." Accessed March 24, 2020. http://www.laurenceanthony.net.

Baker, Paul, Hardie, Andrew, and McEnery, Tony. 2006. *A glossary of corpus linguistics*. Edinburgh: Edinburgh University Press.

Baker, Paul, and McEnery, Tony. 2015. "Introduction". In *Corpora and discourse studies. Integrating discourse and corpora*, edited by Paul Baker and Tony McEnery, 1-19. London: Palgrave Macmillan.

Baker, Paul, and Egbert, Jesse, eds. 2016. *Triangulating methodological approaches in corpus-linguistic research*. London: Routledge.

Barrington, Donal. 1987. "The Constitution in the Courts". *Administration*, No. 35/4: 110-127.

Bates, T. St. John N. 2009. "Different approaches to legislative drafting in the EU Member States". Accessed March 24, 2020. http://www.sigmaweb.org/publicationsdocuments/44577527.pdf.

Bhatia, Vijay K. 1993. *Analysing genre: Language use in professional settings*. London: Longman.

Biber, Douglas. 2006. *University language. A corpus-based study of spoken and written registers.* Amsterdam: Benjamins.

Biber, Douglas, Johansson, Stig, Leech, Geoffrey, Conrad, Susan, and Finegan, Edward. 1999. *Longman grammar of spoken and written English*. London: Longman.

Burke, Ray. 2018. "The Sunday Press: De Valera's 'Irish Ireland' weekly". In *The Sunday papers. A history of Ireland's weekly press*, edited by Joe Breen and Mark O'Brien, 79-97. Dublin: Four Courts.

Bustamante, Thomas. 2013. "On the *argumentum ad absurdum* in statutory interpretation: Its uses and normative significance". In *Legal argumentation theory: Cross-disciplinary perspectives*, edited by Christian Dahlman and Eveline T. Feteris, 21-44. Dordrecht: Springer.

Byrne, Raymond, McCutcheon, Paul, Bruton, Claire, and Coffey, Gerard. 2014. *The Irish legal system*. Dublin: Bloomsbury.

Cahillane, Laura. 2011. "The influence of post-war European constitutions on the Constitution of the Irish Free State". *European Journal of Comparative Law*, No. 15. Accessed March 23, 2020. http://www.ecjcl.org/151/art151-3.pdf.

Carbonell, Flavia. 2013. "Reasoning by consequences: Applying different argumentation structures to the analysis of consequentialist reasoning in judicial decisions". In *Legal argumentation theory: Cross-disciplinary perspectives*, edited by Christian Dahlman and Eveline T. Feteris, 1-20. Dordrecht: Springer.

Casey, James. 2000. *Constitutional law in Ireland*. Dublin: Round Hall Sweet & Maxwell.

Cheng, Winnie. 2012. *Exploring corpus linguistics. Language in action*. London: Routledge.

Chubb, Basil. 1991. *The politics of the Irish Constitution*. Dublin: Institute of Public Administration.

Clarke, Desmond M. 2008. "Interpreting the Constitution: Essentially contested concepts". In *The Irish Constitution: Governance and values*, edited by Oran Doyle and Eoin Carolan, 98-113. Dublin: Thomson Round Hall.

Coakley, John, and Gallagher, Michael, eds. 2005. *Politics in the Republic of Ireland*. London: Routledge.

Conboy, Martin. 2006. *Tabloid Britain: Constructing a community through language*. London: Routledge.

Constitution of the Irish Free State Act, 1922. 1936 [1922]. Dublin: The Stationery Office.

Constitution of Ireland–*Bunreacht na hÉireann*. 1937. Accessed February 27, 2020. https://celt.ucc.ie/published/E900003-005/text002.html.

Constitution of Ireland–*Bunreacht na hÉireann*. 2018 [1937]. Dublin: The Stationery Office.

Crystal David, and Davy, Derek. 1969. *Investigating English style*. London: Longman.

Daly, Mary E. 1994 [1984]. "An Irish Ireland for business?: The Control of Manufacturers Acts, 1932 and 1934". In *The economic development of Ireland since 1870*, edited by Cormac Ó Gráda, 249-275. Vol. 1. Aldershot: Elgar.

Daly, Paul. 2020. "A sound Constitution". Review of *The making of the Irish Constitution 1937–Bunreacht na hÉireann*, by Dermot Keogh and Andrew J. McCarthy. *Dublin Review of Books*, February 2020. [https://www.drb.ie/essays/a-sound-constitution].

Doyle, Oran. 2008. *Constitutional law: Text, cases and materials*. Dublin: Clarus Press.

Egbert, Jesse, and Baker, Paul. 2016. "Research synthesis". In *Triangulating methodological approaches in corpus-linguistic research*, edited by Paul Baker and Jesse Egberts, 183-208. London: Routledge.

Elgie, Robert, and Fitzgerald, Peter. 2005. "The President and the Taoiseach". In *Politics in the Republic of Ireland*, edited by John Coakley and Michael Gallagher, 305-327. London: Routledge.

Ferriter, Diarmaid. 2005. *The transformation of Ireland 1900-2000*. London: Profile Books.

Feteris, Eveline T. 2002. "A pragma-dialectical approach of the analysis and evaluation of pragmatic argumentation in a legal context". *Argumentation*, No. 16: 349-367.

Feteris, Eveline T. 2016. "Prototypical argumentative patterns in a legal context: The role of pragmatic argumentation in the justification of judicial decisions". *Argumentation*, No. 30: 61-79.

Fitzpatrick, David. 1992. "Ireland since 1870". In *The Oxford History of Ireland*, edited by Roy F. Foster, 174-229. Oxford: Oxford University Press.

Flower, Robin. 1947. *The Irish tradition*. Oxford: Clarendon Press.

Flynn, Leo. 1988. "To be an Irish man–Constructions of masculinity within the Constitution". In *Ireland's evolving Constitution 1937-1997*, edited by Tim Murphy and Patrick Twomey, 135-145. London: Hart.

Foley, Michael. 2004. "Colonialism and journalism in Ireland". *Journalism Studies*, No. 5/3: 373-385.

Fürsich, Elfriede. 2009. "In defense of textual analysis. Restoring a challenged method for journalism and media studies". *Journalism Studies*, No. 10/2: 238-252.

Gallagher, Michael. 2005. "The constitution and the judiciary". In *Politics in the Republic of Ireland*, edited by John Coakley and Michael Gallagher, 72-101. London: Routledge.

Garzone, Giuliana. 2001. "Deontic modality and performativity in English legal texts". In *Modality in specialized texts*, edited by Maurizio Gotti and Marina Dossena, 153-174. Bern: Peter Lang.

Glandon, Virginia. 1985. *Arthur Griffith and the advanced-nationalist press, 1900-1922*. New York: Peter Lang.

Gozdz-Roszkowski, Stanislaw. 2011. *Patterns of linguistic Variation in American legal English: A corpus-based study*. Bern: Peter Lang.

Gozdz-Roszkowski, Stanislaw. 2018. "Facts in law: A comparative study of *fact that* and its phraseologies in American and Polish judicial discourse". In *Phraseology in legal and institutional settings. A corpus-based interdisciplinary perspective*, edited by Stanislaw Gozdz-Roszkowski and Gianluca Pontrandolfo, 143-159. London: Routledge.

Hannon, Paul. 2008. "In God's name, what next? Religion, the Constitution and the new Ireland". In *The Irish Constitution: Governance and values*, edited by Oran Doyle and Eoin Carolan, 463-475. Dublin: Thomson Round Hall.

Happer, Catherine, and Philo, Greg. 2013. "The role of the media in the construction of public belief and social change". *Journal of Social and Political Psychology*, No. 1/1: 321-336.

Hogan, Gerard. 1987. "Constitutional interpretation". *Administration*, No. 35/4: 173-191.

Holmes, David G. 2000. "The Eucharistic Congress of 1932 and Irish identity". *New Hibernia Review/Iris Éireannach Nua*, No. 4/1: 55-78.

Hunston, Susan, and Francis, Gill. 1998. "Verbs observed: a corpus-driven pedagogic grammar". *Applied Linguistics*, No. 19: 45-72.

Kee, Robert. 2000 [1972]. *The green flag. A history of Irish nationalism*. London: Penguin.

Kelly, John M. 1988. "Fundamental rights and the Constitution". In *De Valera's Constitution and ours*, edited by Brian Farrell, 163-173. Dublin: Gill & MacMillan.

Kelly, John M. 1994 [1961]. *The Irish Constitution*. Dublin: Butterworths.

Keogh, Dermot, and McCarthy, Andrew J. 2007. *The making of the Irish Constitution 1937–Bunreacht na hÉireann*. Cork: Mercier Press.

Kissane, Bill. 2002. *Explaining Irish democracy*. Dublin: University College Dublin Press.

Kloosterhuis, Harm. 2005. "Reconstructing complex analogy argumentation in judicial decisions: A pragma-dialectical perspective". *Argumentation*, No. 19: 471-483.

Larkin, Felix M. 2012. "No longer a political side show: T. R. Harrington and the 'new' Irish Independent". In *Independent newspapers. A history*, edited by Mark O'Brien and Kevin Rafter, 26-38. Dublin: Four Courts Press.

Lee, John J. 1989. *Ireland, 1912-1985: Politics and society*. Cambridge: Cambridge University Press.

Locke, John. 2017 [1690]. *An essay concerning human understanding*. Accessed December 2, 2019. https://www.earlymoderntexts.com/assets/pdfs/locke1690book1.pdf.

Mac Cormaic, Ruadhán. 2016. *The Supreme Court*. London: Penguin.

MacCormick, Neil. 1978. "The motivation of judgments in the common law". In *La motivation des décisions de justice*, edited by Chaïm Perelman and Paul Foriers, 167-194. Bruxelles: Bruylant.

Madison, James. 1787. "The Federalist No. L: On maintaining a just partition of power among the necessary departments". In *The Federalist*, edited by Alexander Hamilton, John Jay and James Madison, 284-288. New York: The Colonial Press.

Mattila, Heikki. E. S. 2013. *Comparative legal linguistics. Language of law, Latin and modern Lingua Francas*. Farnham: Ashgate.

Maume, Patrick. 2004. "The *Irish Independent* and Empire, 1891-1919". In *Newspapers and Empire in Ireland and Britain: Reporting the British Empire, c. 1857-1921*, edited by Simon Potter, 124-142. Dublin: Four Courts Press.

Mazzi, Davide. 2007. *The linguistic study of judicial argumentation: Theoretical perspectives, analytical insights.* Modena: Il Fiorino.

Mazzi, Davide. 2010. "The centrality of counterfactual conditionals in House of Lords and US Supreme Court judgments". In *Legal discourse across languages and cultures*, edited by Maurizio Gotti and Christopher Williams, 243-262. Bern: Peter Lang.

Mazzi, Davide. 2016. *The Theoretical background and practical implications of argumentation in Ireland.* Newcastle upon Tyne: Cambridge Scholars Publishing.

Mazzi, Davide. 2018. "Phraseology, argumentation and identity in Supreme Court of Ireland's judgments on language policy". *Journal of Applied Linguistics and Professional Practice*, No. 11/3: 315-337.

Mazzi, Davide. 2019. *Views of place, views of Irishness. Representing the Gaeltacht in the Irish Press, 1895-1905*. Oxford: Peter Lang.

Mazzi, Davide. Forthcoming. "'If you want Ireland to prosper...': A discourse-analytic study of Irishness in advertising from the 1930s". In *The role of context in the production and reception of historical news discourse*, edited by Nicholas Brownlees. Bern: Peter Lang.

McDonagh, Enda. 1987. "Philosophical-theological reflections on the Constitution". *Administration*, No. 35/4: 192-205.

McEnery, Tony, and Wilson, Andrew. 1996. *Corpus linguistics*. Edinburgh: Edinburgh University Press.

Mellinkoff, David. 1963. *The language of the law*. Boston: Little, Brown & Co.

Morash, Christopher. 2010. *A history of the media in Ireland*. Cambridge: Cambridge University Press.

Morgan, David G. 1998. "Judicial activism: Too much of a good thing?". In *The Irish Constitution: Governance and values*, edited by Oran Doyle and Eoin Carolan, 109-119. Dublin: Thomson Round Hall.

Morgan, David G. 2001. *A judgment too far? Judicial activism & the Constitution*. Cork: Cork University Press.

Moynihan, Maurice. 1980. *Speeches and statements by Eamon de Valera*. Dublin: Gill & Macmillan.

Murphy, William M. 1909. *The story of a newspaper*. Dublin: Irish Independent.

Neary, J. Peter, and Ó Gráda, Cormac. 1991. "Protection, economic war and structural change: The 1930s in Ireland". *Irish Historical Studies*, No. 27: 250-266.

Nivelle, Nele, and Van Belle, William. 2007. "The use of counterfactual conditionals expressing causation in legal discourse". In *Proceedings of the sixth conference of the International Society for the Study of Argumentation*, edited by Frans H. Van Eemeren, Anthony J. Blair, Charles A. Willard and Bart Garssen, 989-996. Amsterdam: SicSat.

Noguchi, Judy, Orr, Thomas, and Tono, Yukio. 2006. "Using a dedicated corpus to identify features of professional English usage: What do "we" do in science journal articles?". In *Corpus linguistics around the world*, edited by Andrew Wilson, Dawn Archer and Paul Rayson, 155-166. Amsterdam: Rodopi.

O'Brien, Mark. 2001. *De Valera, Fianna Fáil and the Irish Press*. Dublin: Irish Academic Press.

Ó Cearúil, Micheál. 1999. *Bunreacht na hÉireann. A study of the Irish text*. Dublin: Stationery Office of the Government of Ireland.

Ó Dónaill, Niall. 1977. *Foclóir Gaeilge-Béarla*. Dublin: An Gúm.

O'Rourke, Malachy. 2014. "Inconsistencies in the sources and use of Irish legal terminology". In *Legal lexicography: A comparative perspective*, edited by Máirtín Mac Aodha, 265-287. Farnham: Ashgate.

Palmer, Frank R. 1988. *The English verb*. London: Longman.

Partington, Alan. 2003. *The linguistics of political argument: The spin-doctor and the wolf-pack at the White House*. London: Routledge.

Partington, Alan, Duguid, Alison, and Taylor, Charlotte. 2013. *Patterns and meanings in discourse. Theory and practice in corpus-assisted discourse studies (CADS)*. Amsterdam: Benjamins.

Perelman, Chaïm. 1978. "La motivation des decisions de justice–Essai de synthèse". In *La motivation des décisions de justice*, edited by Chaïm Perelman and Paul Foriers, 415-426. Bruxelles: Bruylant.

Perelman, Chaïm. 1979. *Logica giuridica e nuova retorica*. Milan: Giuffrè.

Perelman, Chaïm. 1980. *Justice, law and argument*. Dordrecht: Reidel.

Pontrandolfo, Gianluca. 2013. "La fraseología como estilema del lenguaje judicial: El caso de las locuciones prepositivas desde una perspectiva contrastiva". In *Discurso profesional y lingüística de corpus. Perspectivas de investigación*, edited by Luisa Chierichetti and Giovanni Garofalo, 187-215. Bergamo: CELSB.

Press, J. P. 1986. "Protectionism and the Irish footwear industry". *Irish Economic and Social History*, No. 13: 74-89.

Rafter, Kevin, ed. 2011. *Irish journalism before independence. More a disease than a profession*. Manchester: Manchester University Press.

Salkie, Raphael. 2018. "Legal phraseology in contrast. *The fact that* and its German counterparts". In *Phraseology in legal and institutional settings. A corpus-based interdisciplinary perspective*, edited by Stanislaw Gozdz-Roszkowski and Gianluca Pontrandolfo, 126-142. London: Routledge.

Scannell, Yvonne. 1988. "The Constitution and the role of women". In *De Valera's Constitution and ours*, edited by Brian Farrell, 123-136. Dublin: Gill & MacMillan.

Scott, Mike. 2010. *WordSmith Tools 5.0*. Liverpool: Lexical Analysis Software.

Sinclair, John. 1991. *Corpus, concordance, collocation*. Oxford: Oxford University Press.

Sinclair, John. 2004. *Trust the text. Language, corpus and discourse*. London: Routledge.

Smyth, Gerry. 2012. "Irish national identity after the Celtic Tiger". *Estudios Irlandeses*, No. 7: 132-137.

Snoeck Henkemans, A. Francisca. 2003. "Complex argumentation in a critical discussion". *Argumentation*, No. 17: 405–419.

Stubbs, Michael. 1996. *Text and corpus analysis: Computer-assisted studies of language and culture*. Oxford: Blackwell.

Stubbs, Michael. 2001. *Words and phrases: Corpus studies on lexical semantics*. Oxford: Blackwell.

Téarmaí Dlí 1960 [1957]. Dublin: Oifig an tSoláthair.

Tiersma, Peter. 2012. "A history of the language of the law". In *The Oxford handbook of language and law*, edited by Lawrence M. Solan and Peter Tiersma, 13-26. Oxford: Oxford University Press.

Tobin, Mary. 2018. "Literacy and society in Ireland 1900-1980". PhD diss., National University of Ireland (Maynooth).

Tognini Bonelli, Elena. 2001. *Corpus linguistics at work*. Amsterdam: Benjamins.

Uí Fhaoláin, Aoife. 2014. "Language revival and conflicting identities in the *Irish Independent*". *Irish Studies Review*, No. 22/1: 63-79.

Van Eemeren, Frans H. 2001. *Crucial concepts in argumentation theory*. Amsterdam: Amsterdam University Press.

Van Eemeren, Frans H. 2010. *Strategic maneuvering in argumentative discourse*. Amsterdam: Benjamins.

Van Eemeren, Frans H. 2011. "In context. Giving contextualization its rightful place in the study of argumentation". *Argumentation*, No. 25: 141-161.

Van Eemeren, Frans H. 2016. "Identifying argumentative patterns: A vital step in the development of pragma-dialectics". *Argumentation*, No. 30: 1-23.

Van Eemeren, Frans H., and Grootendorst, Rob. 1992. *Argumentation, communication, and fallacies*. Hillsdale: Lawrence Erlbaum Associates.

Van Eemeren, Frans H., Grootendorst, Rob, and Snoeck Henkemans, A. Francisca. 2002. *Argumentation. Analysis, evaluation, presentation*. Mahwah, NJ: Lawrence Erlbaum Associates.

Van Eemeren, Frans H., Houtlosser, Peter, and Snoeck Henkemans, A. Francisca. 2007. *Argumentative indicators in discourse. A pragma-dialectical approach*. Dordrecht: Springer.

Van Poppel, Lotte. 2012. "Pragmatic argumentation in health brochures". *Journal of Argumentation in Context*, No. 1: 97-112.

Walsh, Brian J. 1988. "The Constitution: A view from the bench". In *De Valera's Constitution and ours*, edited by Brian Farrell, 188-197. Dublin: Gill & MacMillan.

Walton, Douglas. 2010. "Formalization of the ad hominem argumentation scheme". *Journal of Applied Logic*, No. 8: 1-21.

Whately, Richard. 1853 [1828]. *Elements of rhetoric comprising an analysis of the laws of moral evidence and persuasion with rules for argumentative composition and elocution*. New York: Harper & Brothers.

Whelan, Aoife. 2012. "'Irish Ireland' and the Irish Independent, 1905-22". In *Independent newspapers. A history*, edited by Mark O'Brien and Kevin Rafter, 67-80. Dublin: Four Courts Press.

Williams, Christopher. 2018. "Legal drafting". In *Handbook of communication in the legal sphere*, edited by Jacqueline Visconti, 13-35. Berlin: De Gruyter.

Wray, Alison. 2002. *Formulaic language and the lexicon*. Cambridge: Cambridge University Press.

INDEX